Original
Black & White
Photography

Joseph Fleming

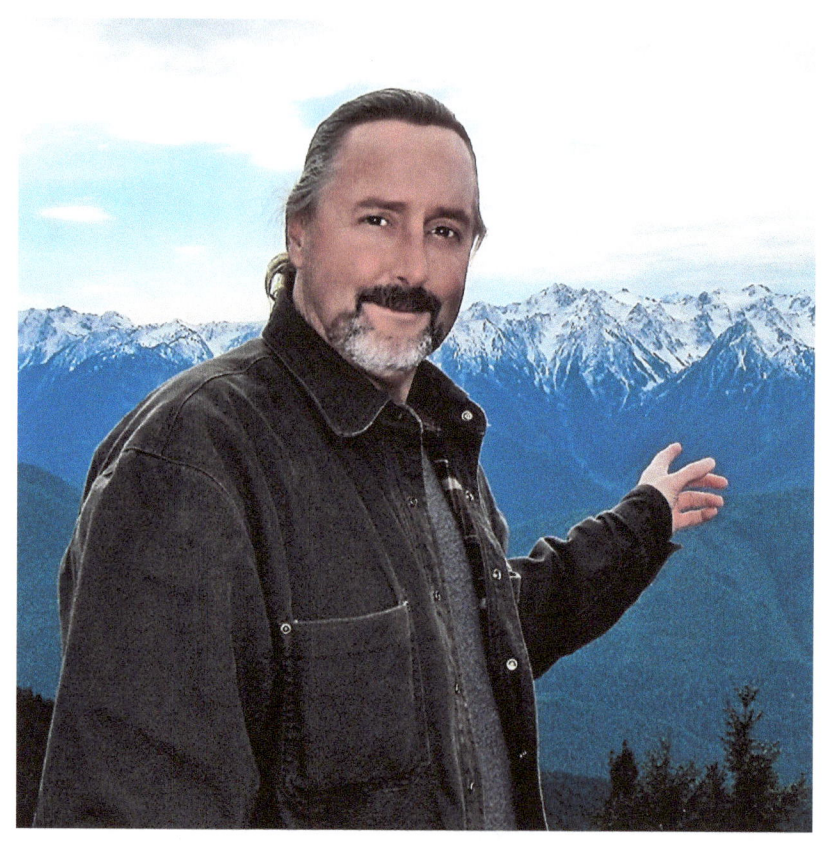

Joseph Fleming

Selected Images
photograph collection

Decades of being around accomplished talent producing absolutely phenomenal quality work has taught that we are capable of greatness. It is possible to meet our destiny and become it. Experiencing excellence done with such apparent ease and humble selfless gratification is the motivation for this photography. Most important was having the freedom

Being colorblind gives an advantage when composing black & white… less confusion.
This special collection selected from thousands of captures. All images were framed
in the camera and presented without edits, genuine as seen through the lens.
RAW conversion applied by proprietary panchromatic process.

Fine art prints from source files. Contact for custom work.

info@ BEACHNOISE.com

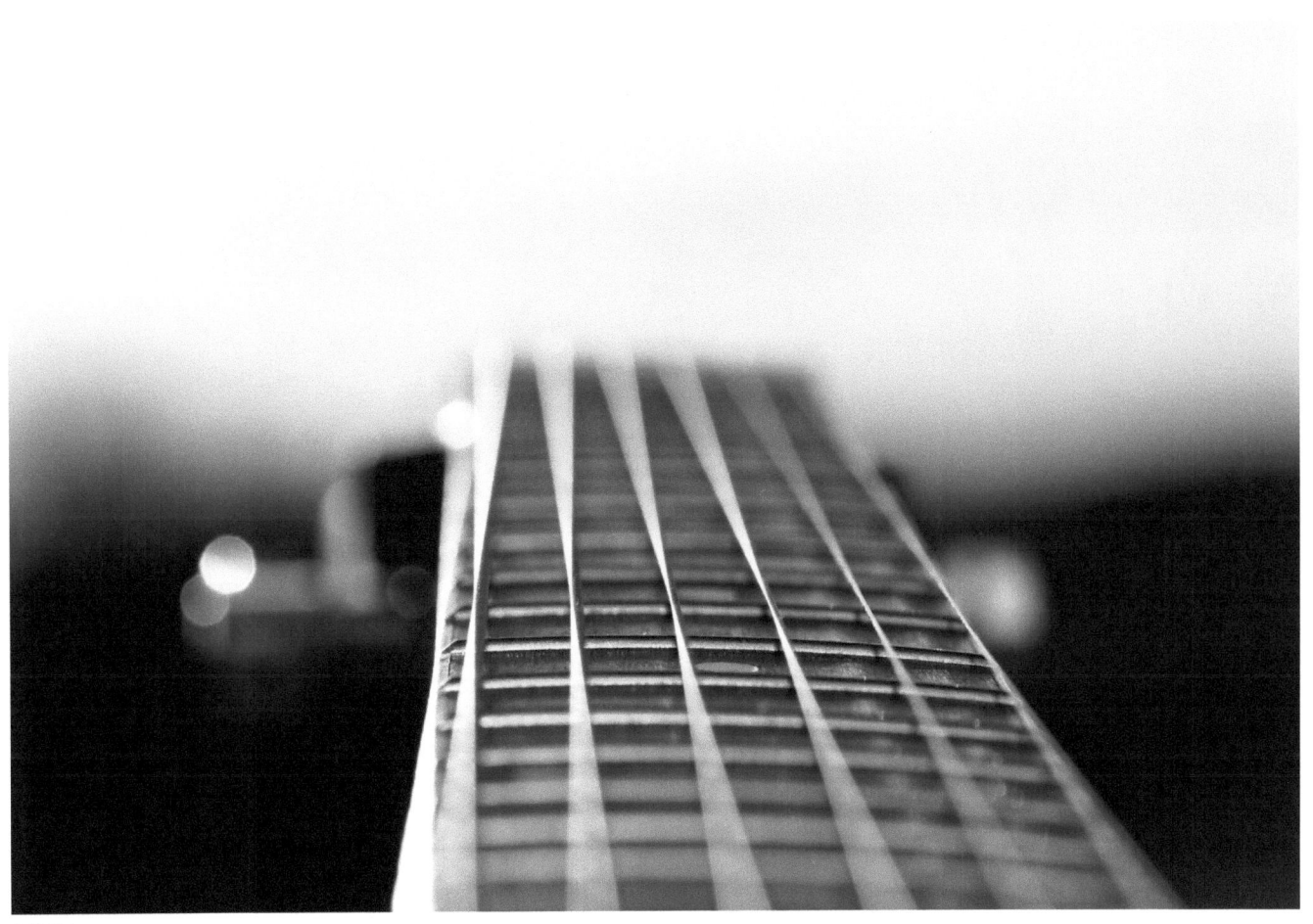

0351

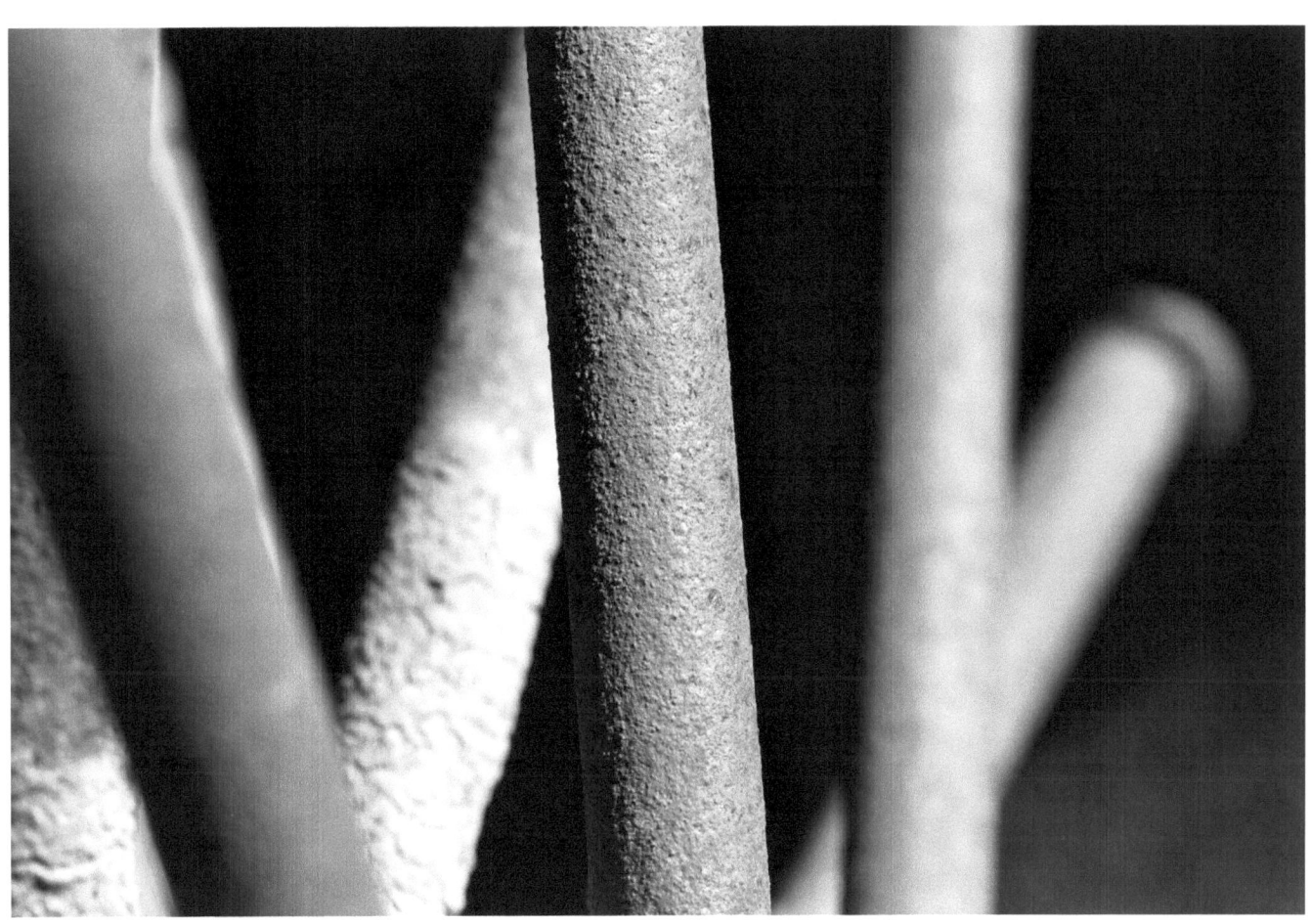

0780

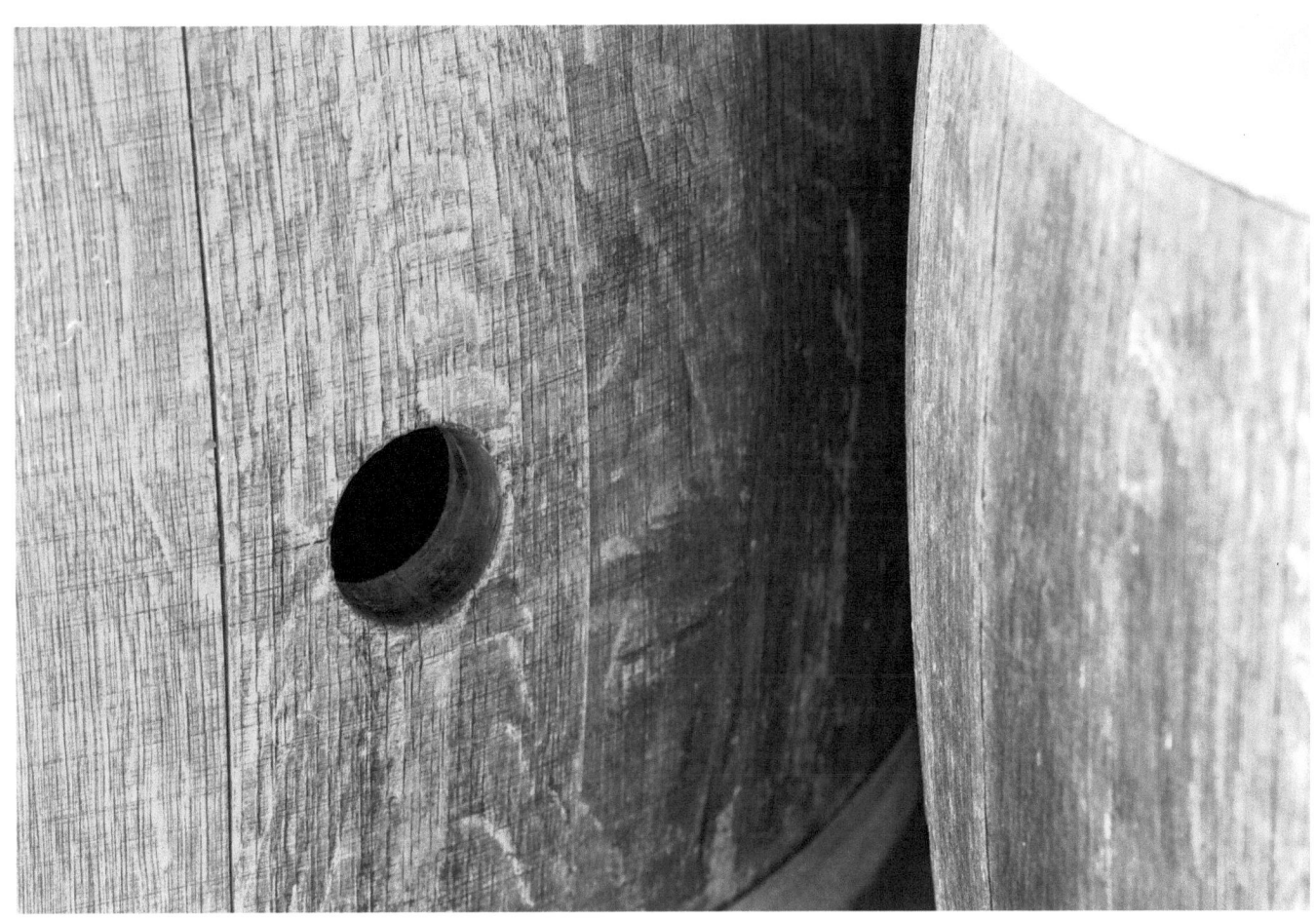

0826

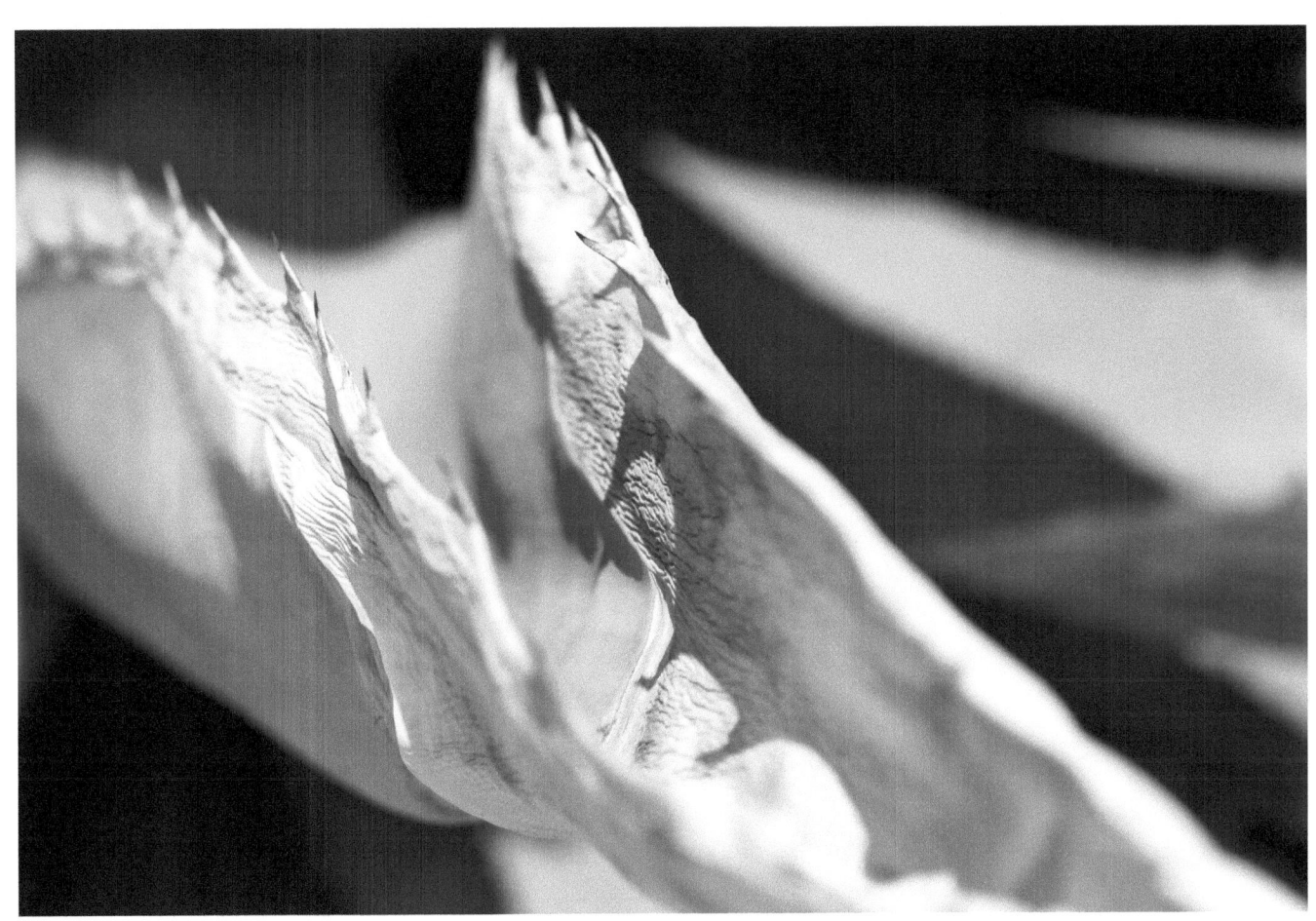

1581

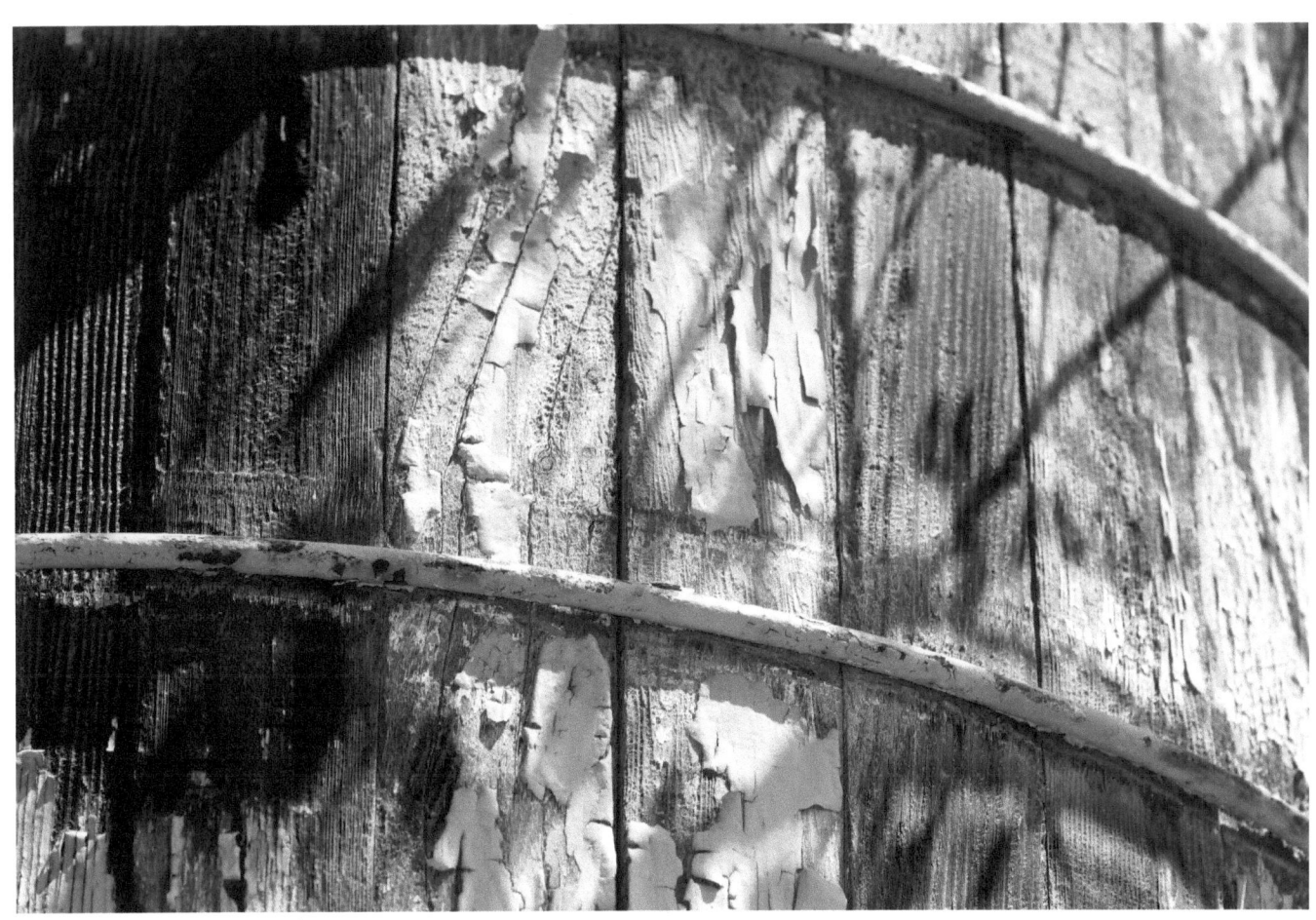

1608

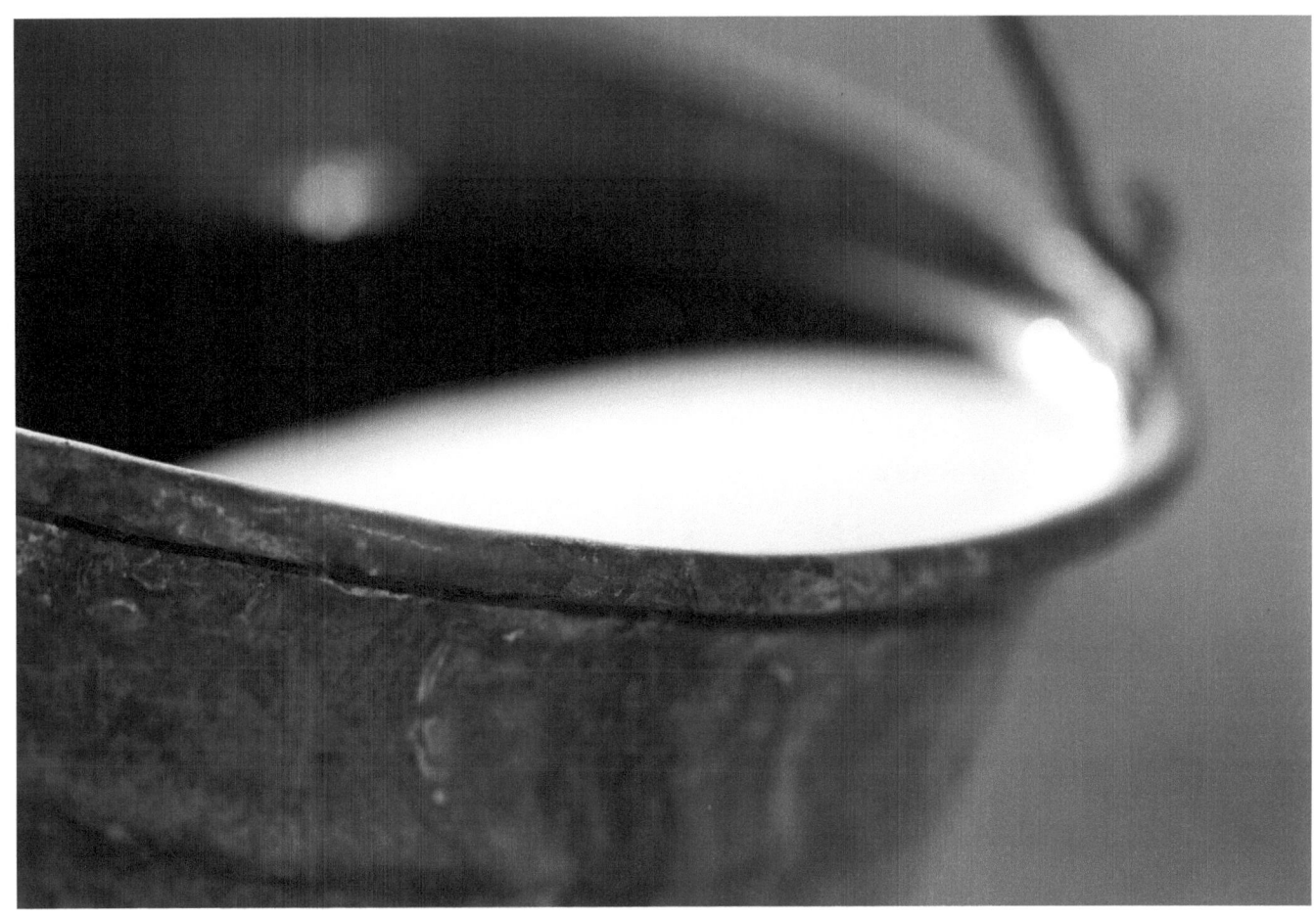

2180

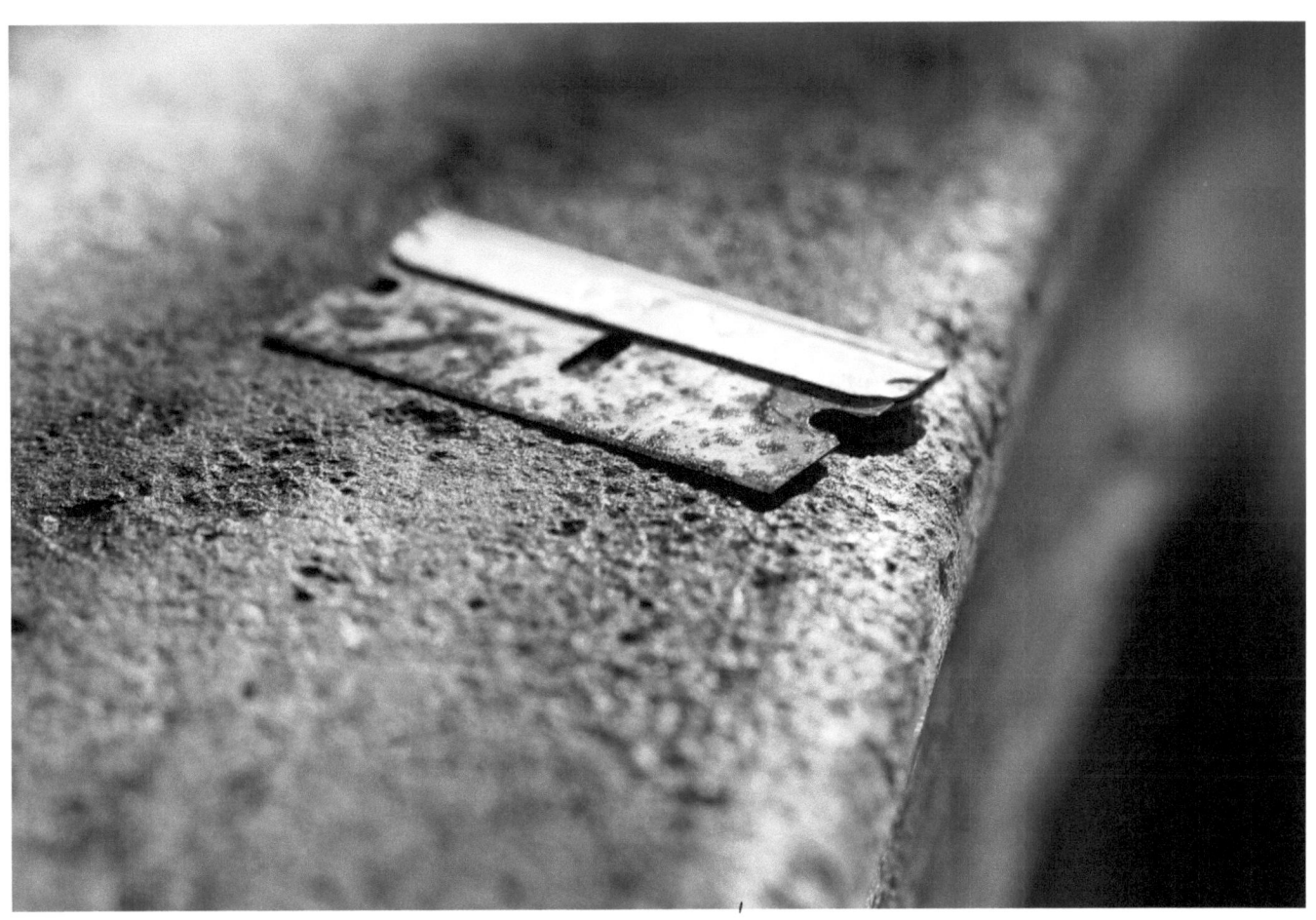

2467

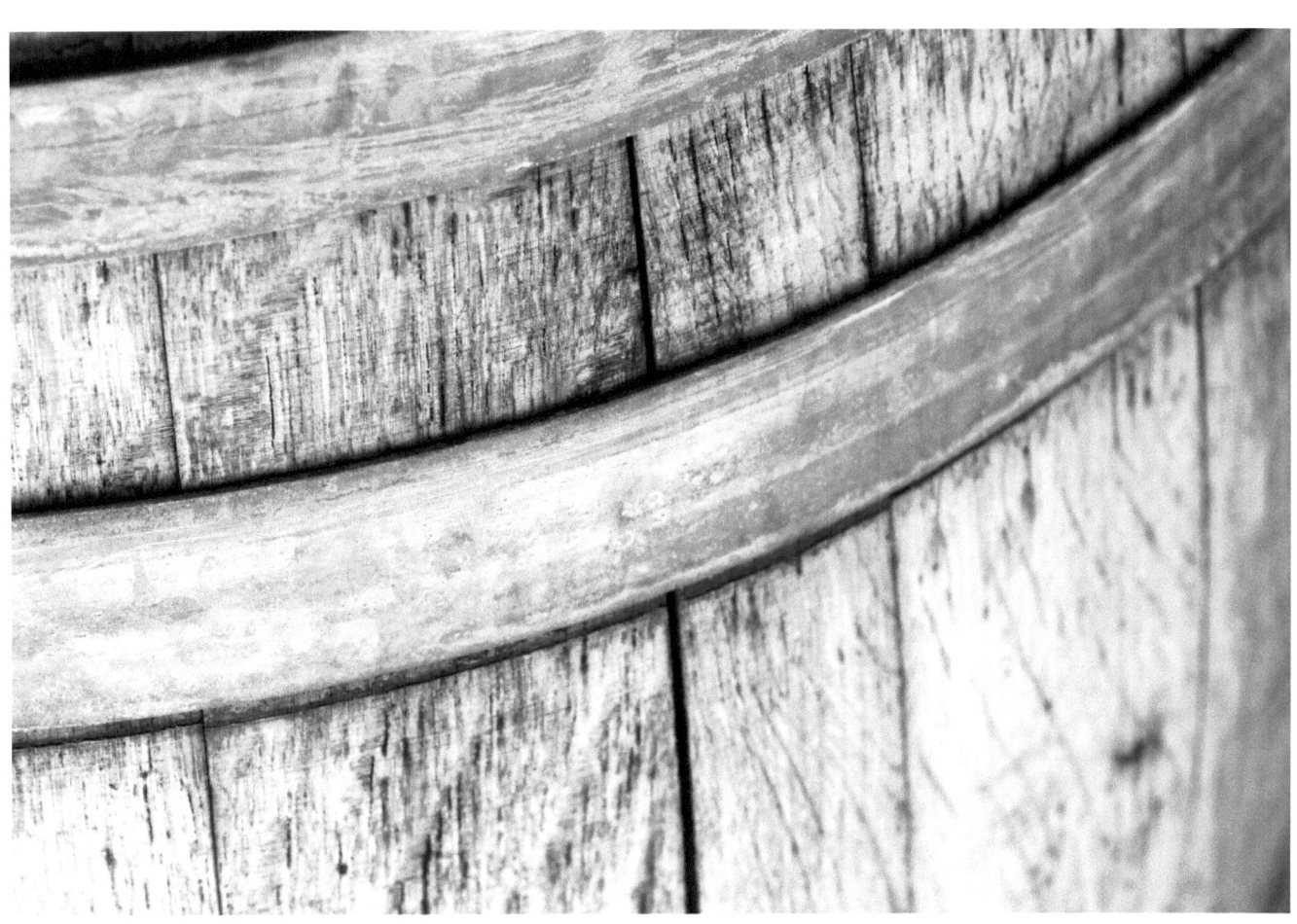

3151

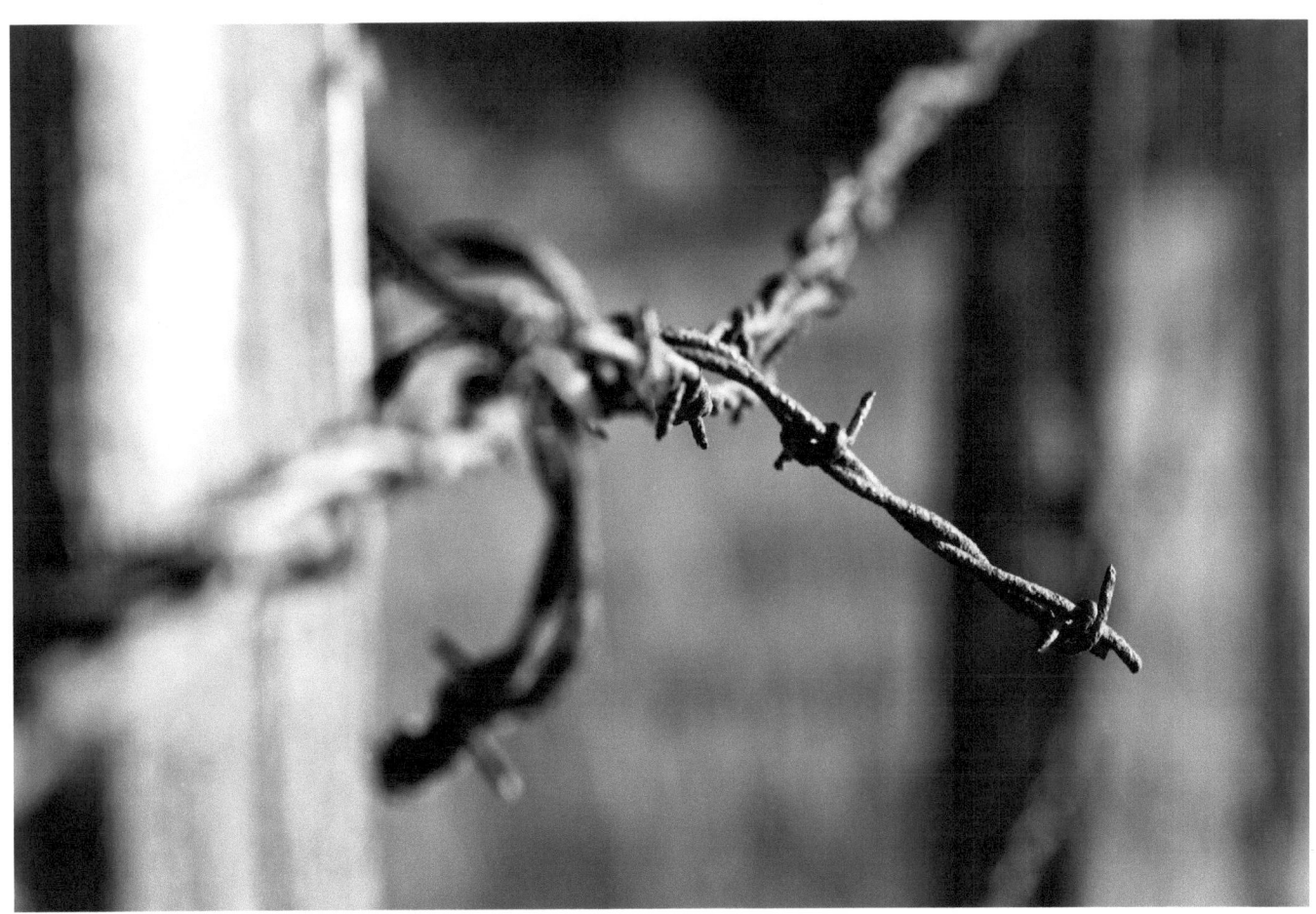

3359

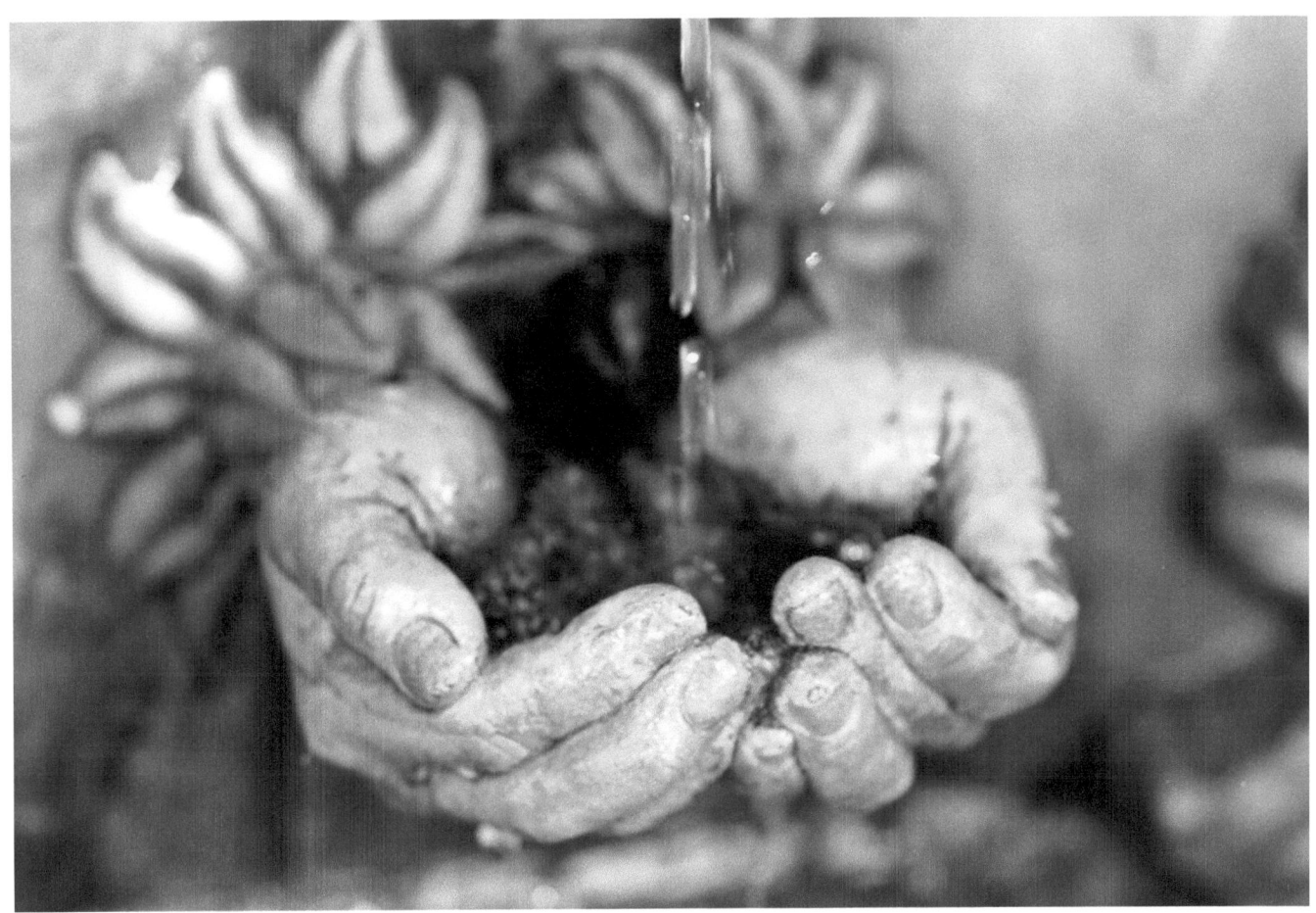

3720

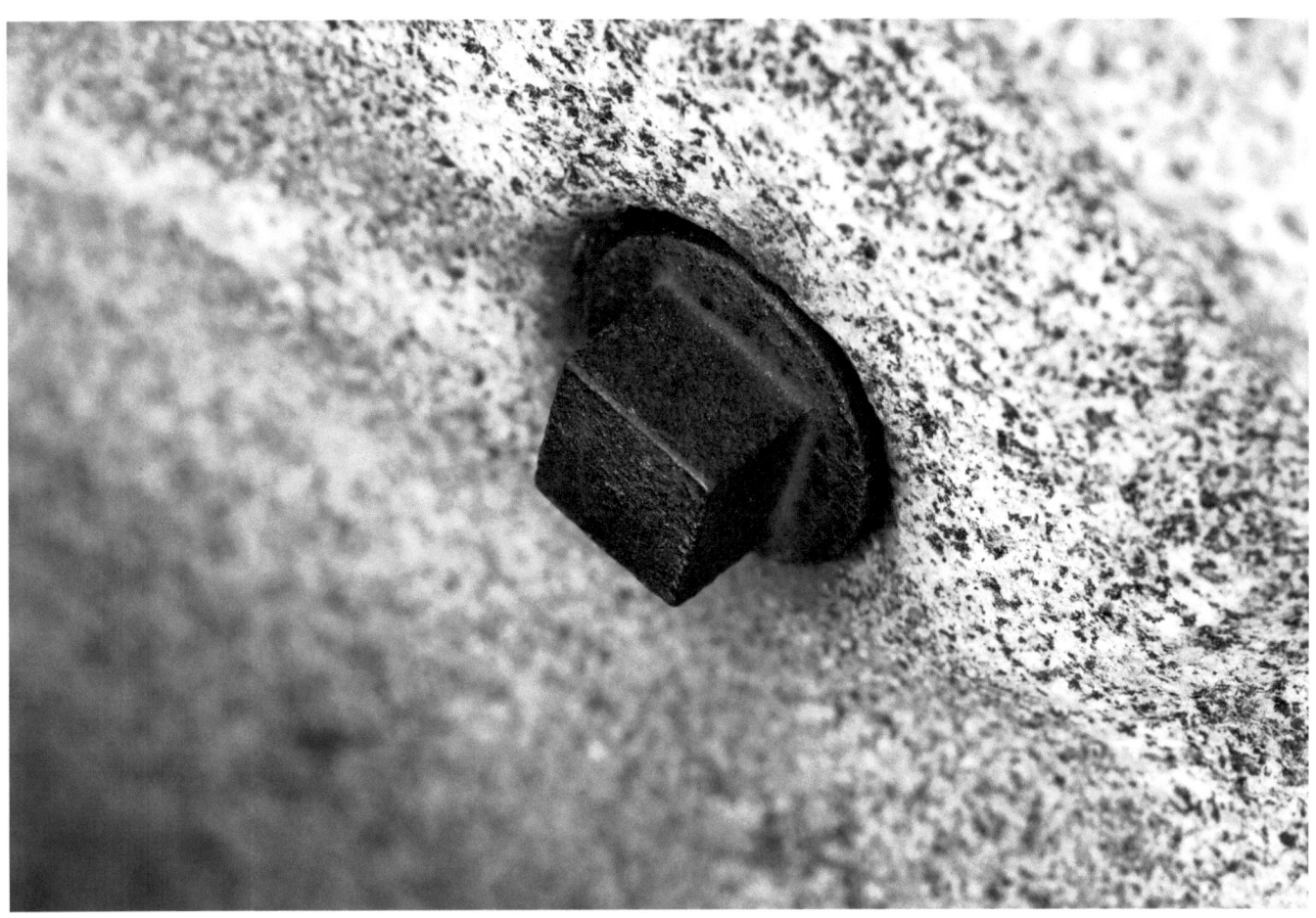

4035

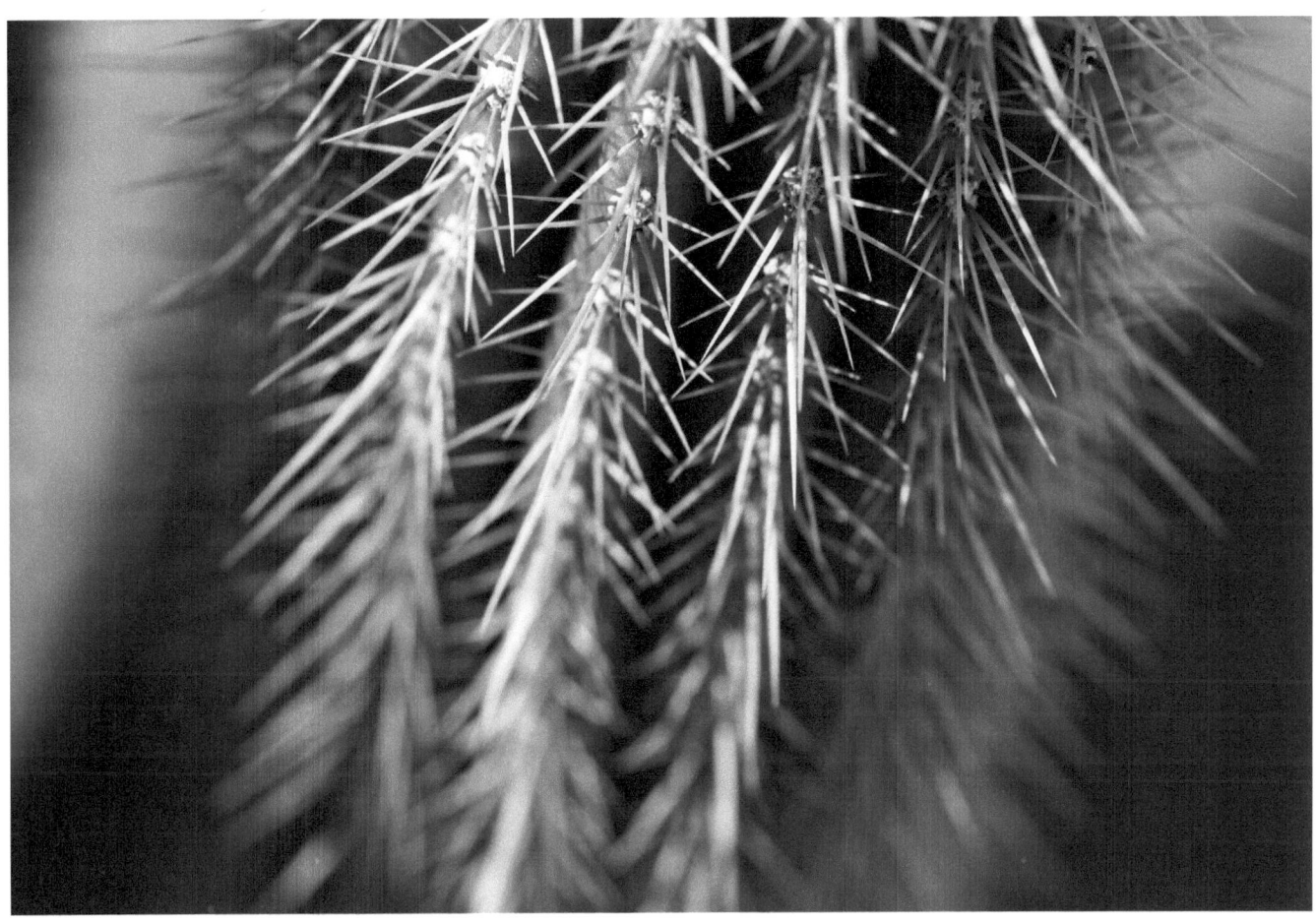

4070

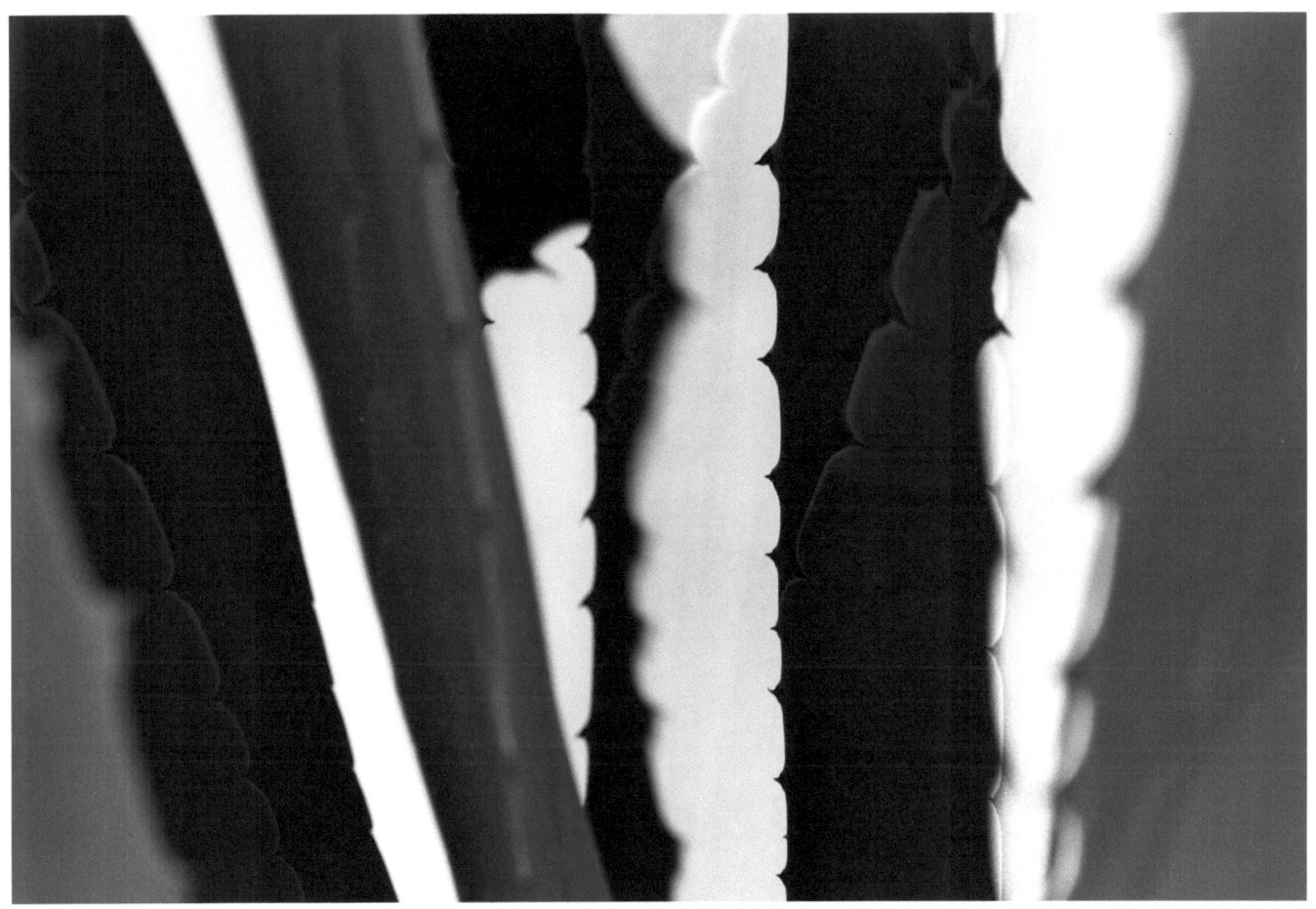

4099

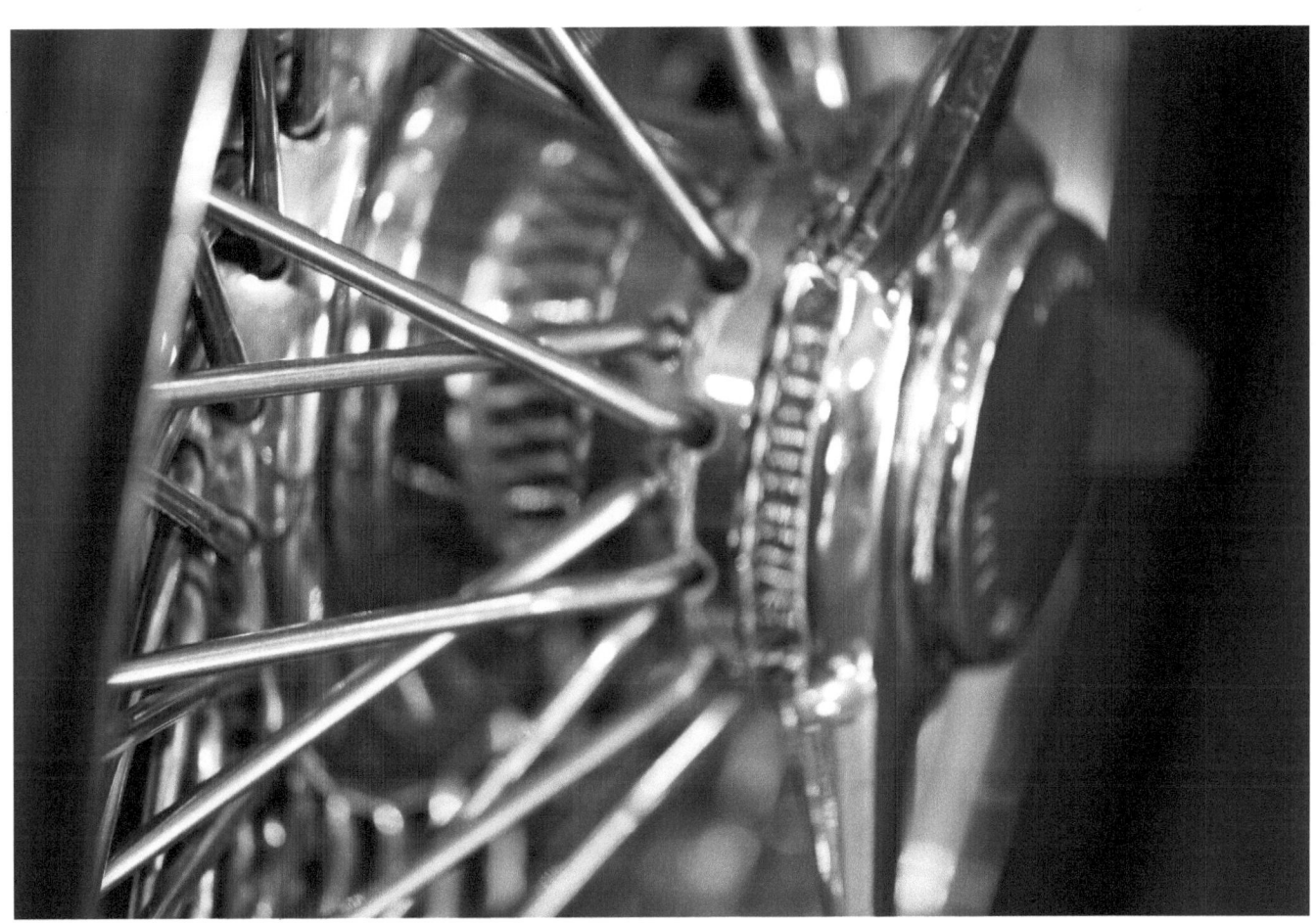

4193

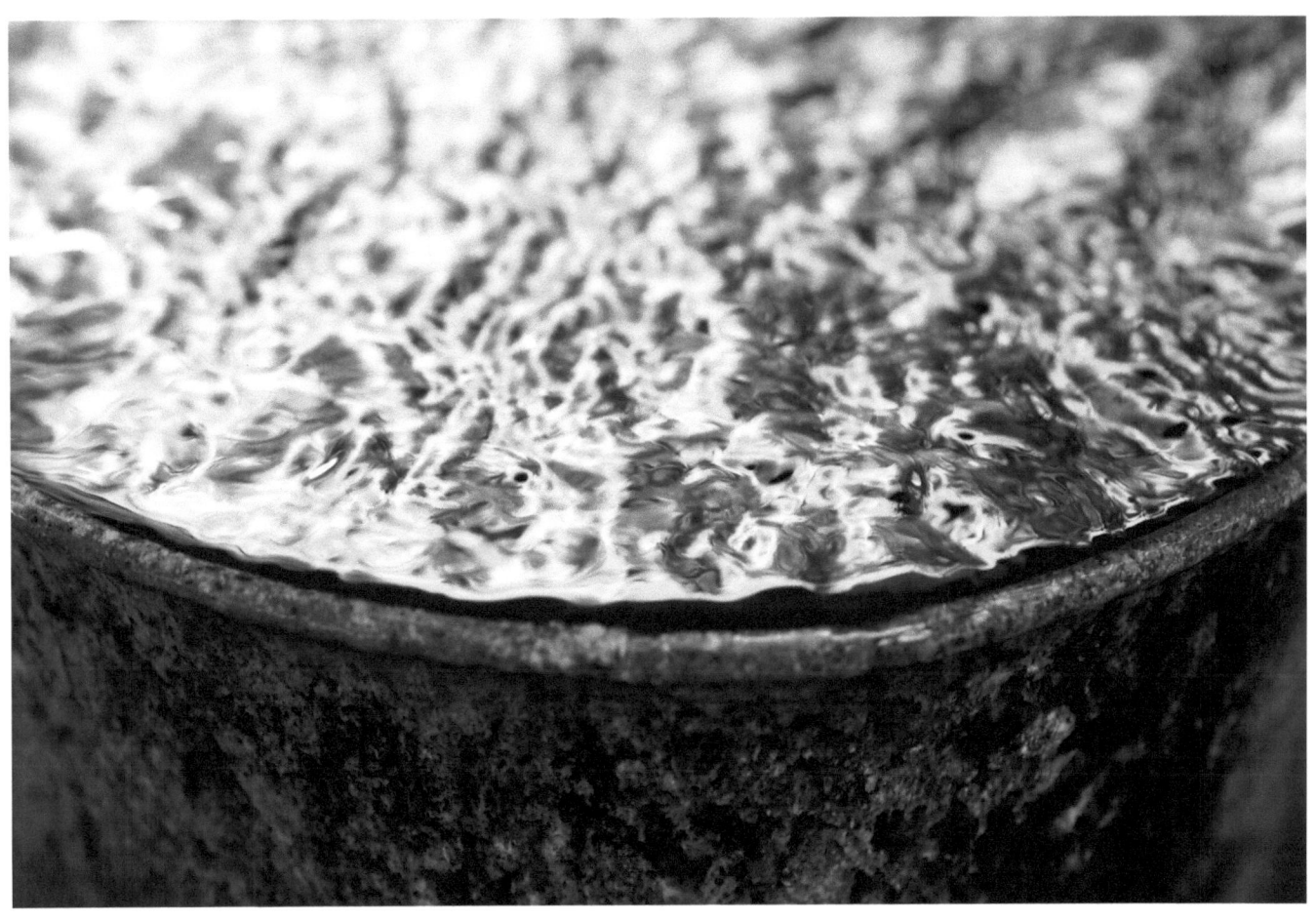

4533

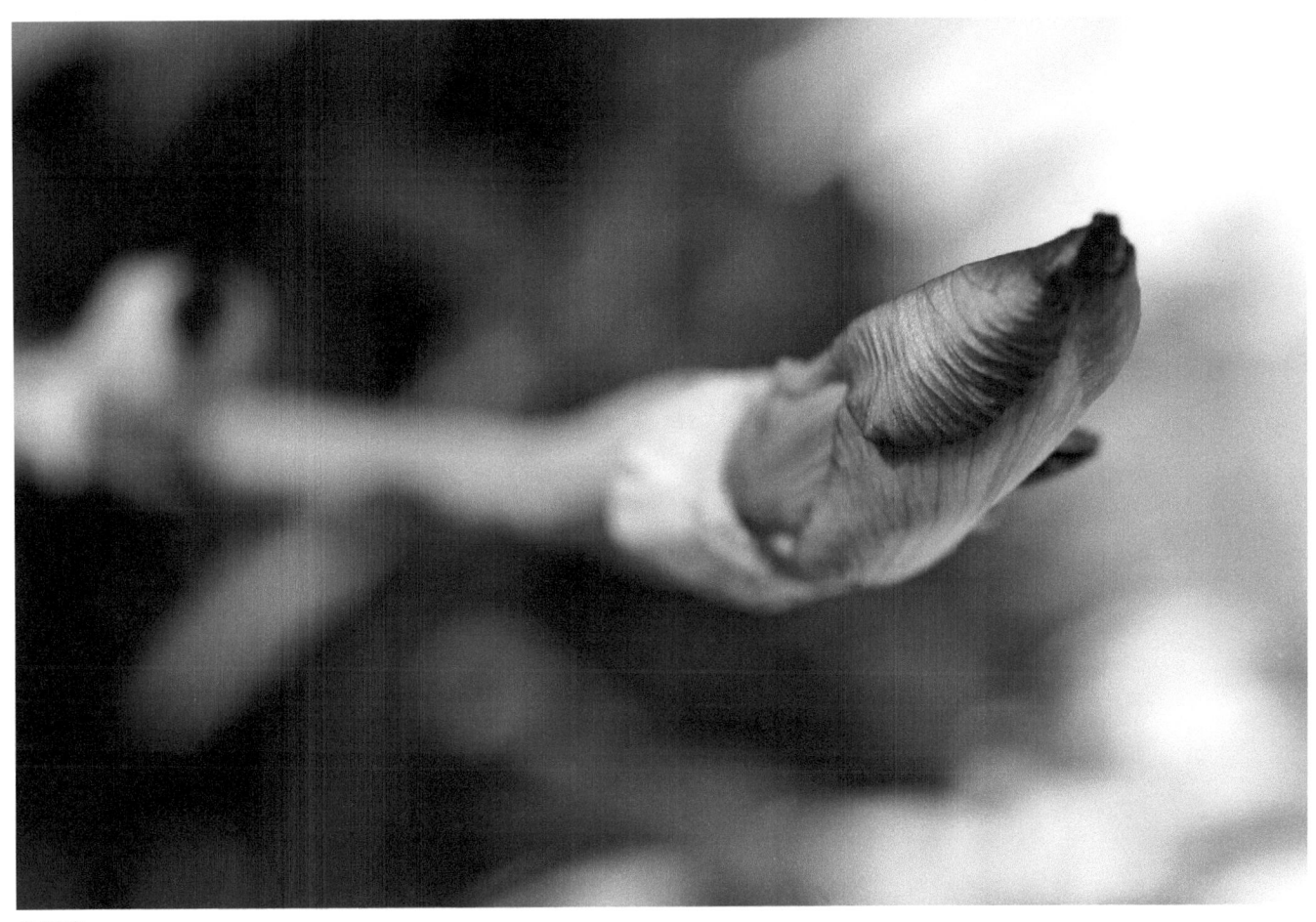

5492

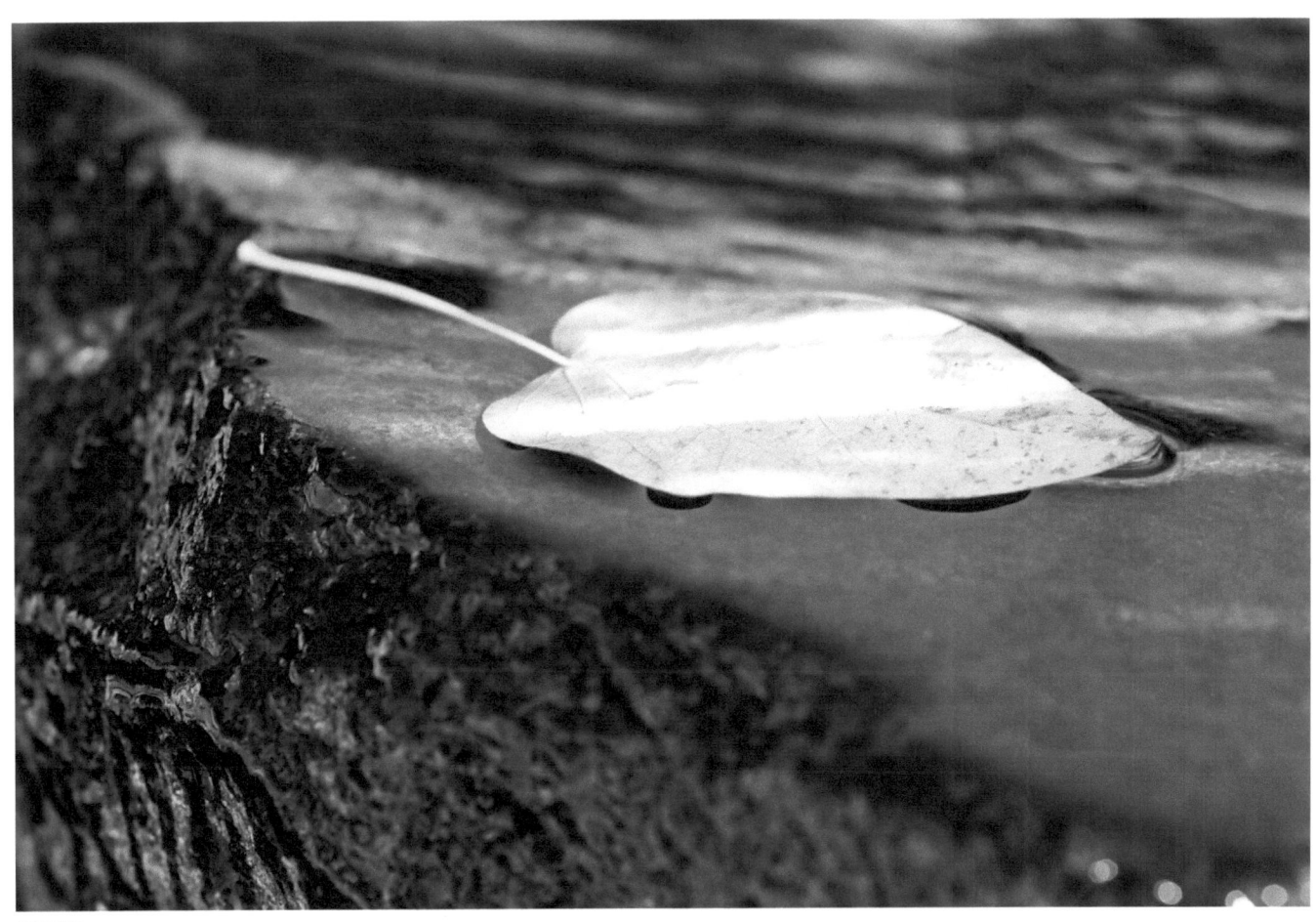

5750

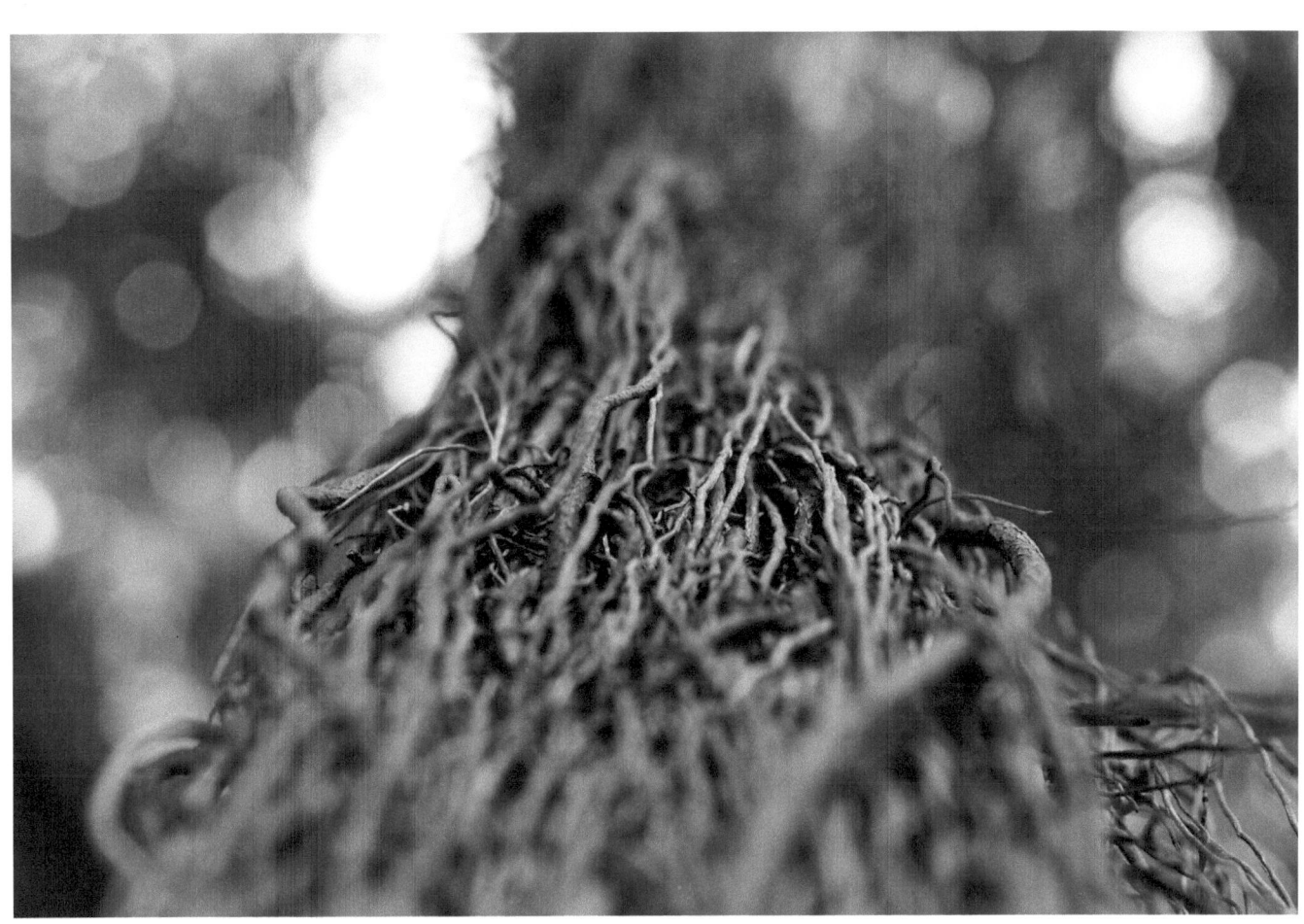

5811

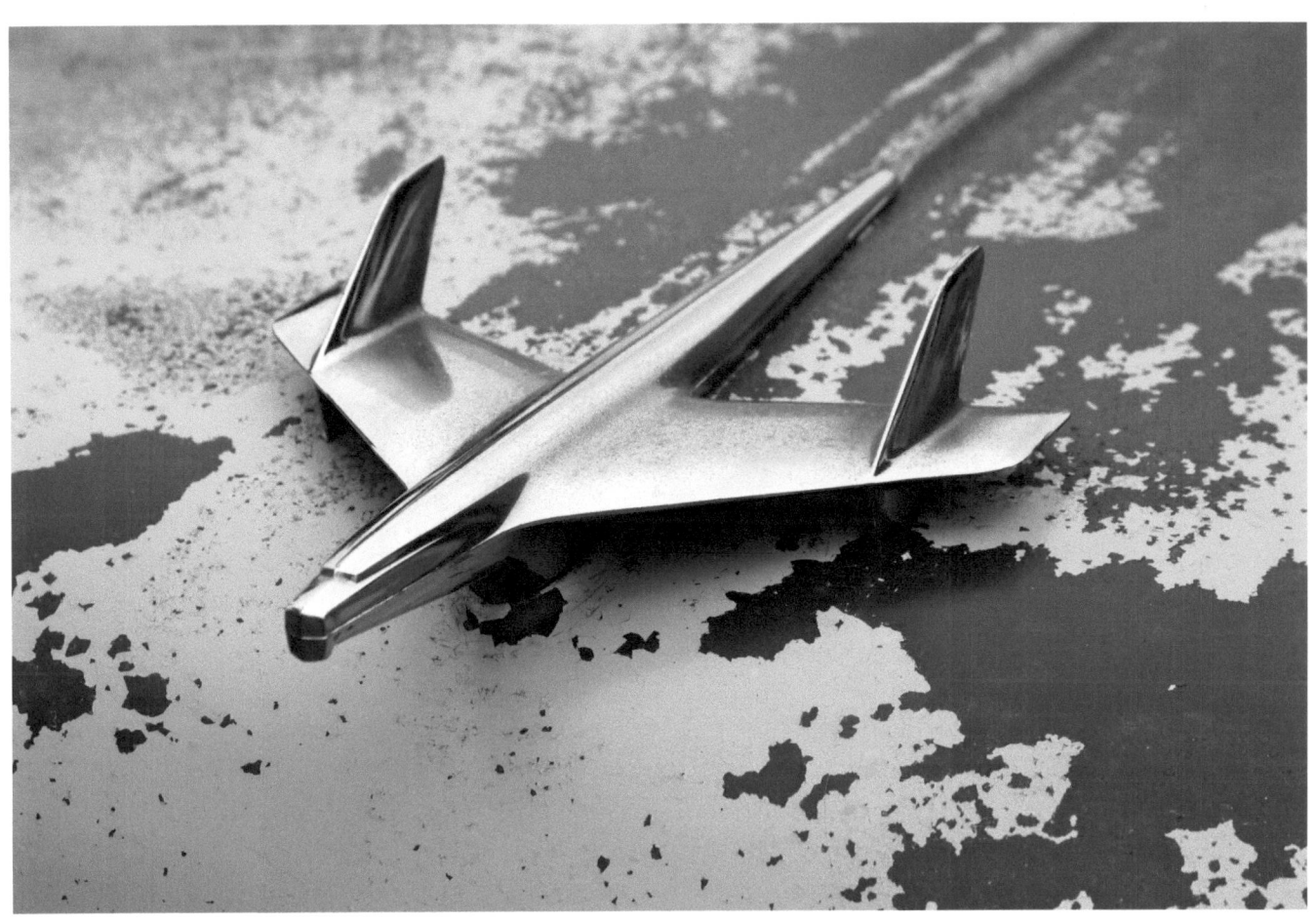

5846

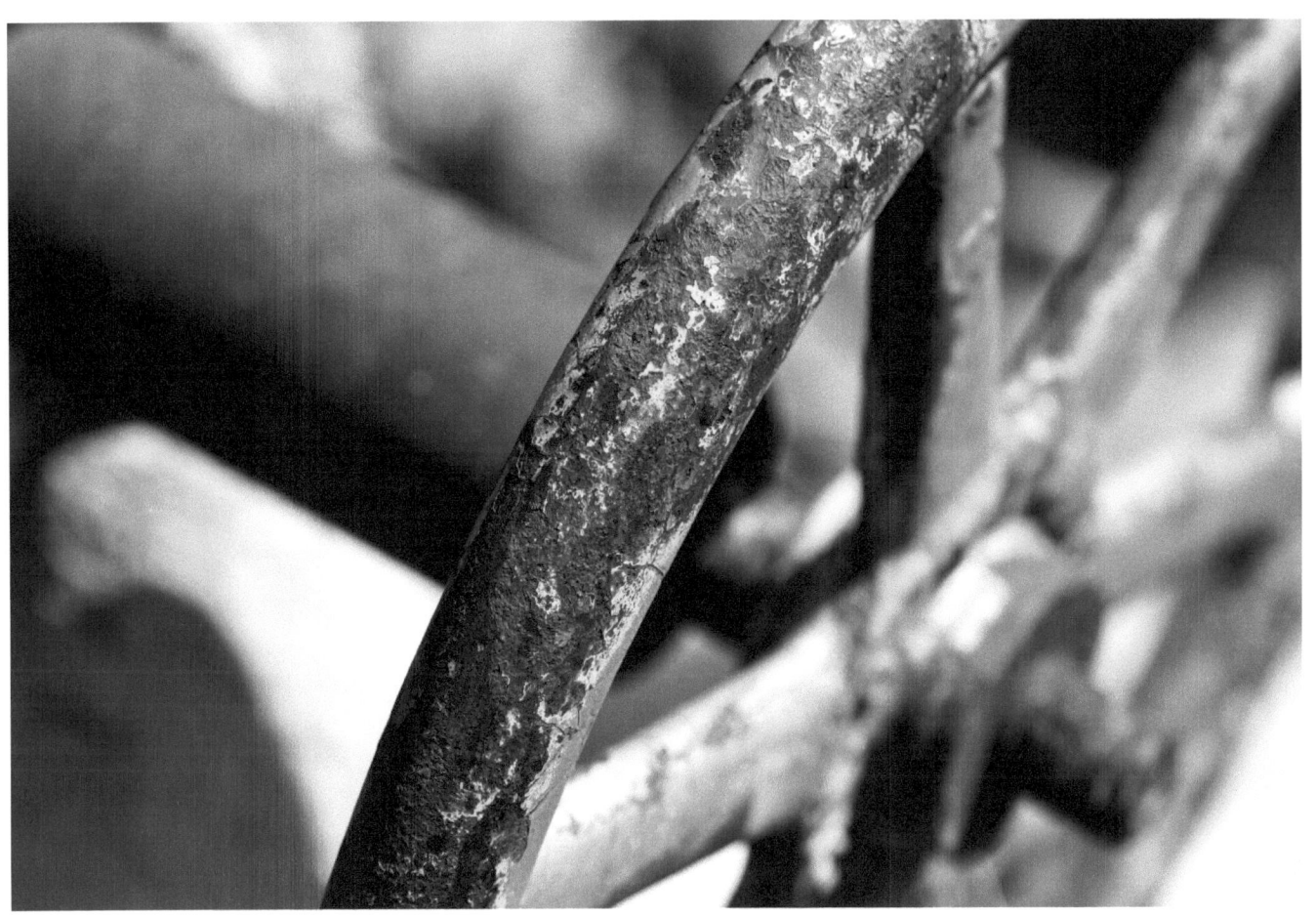

6095

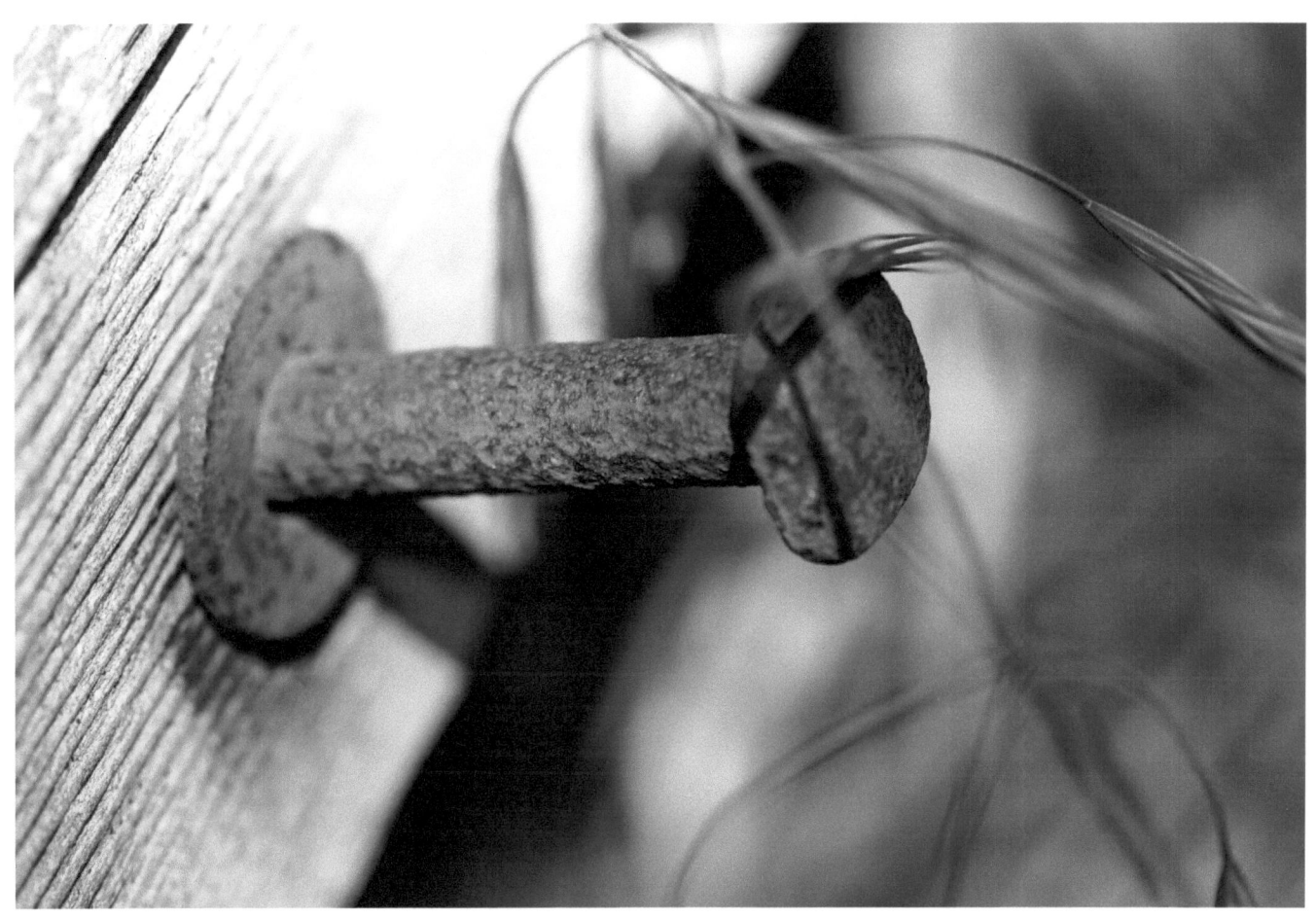

7182

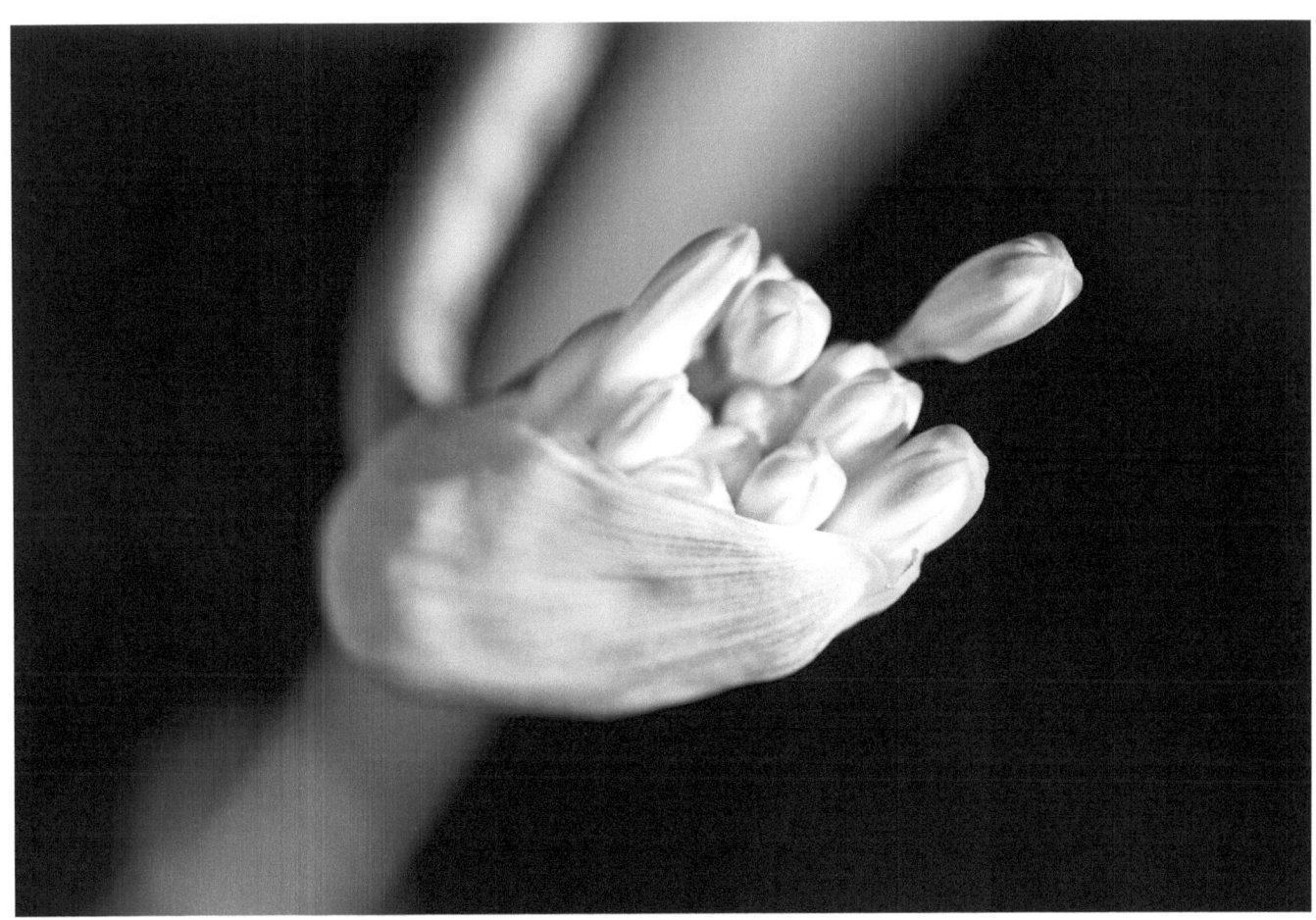

8407

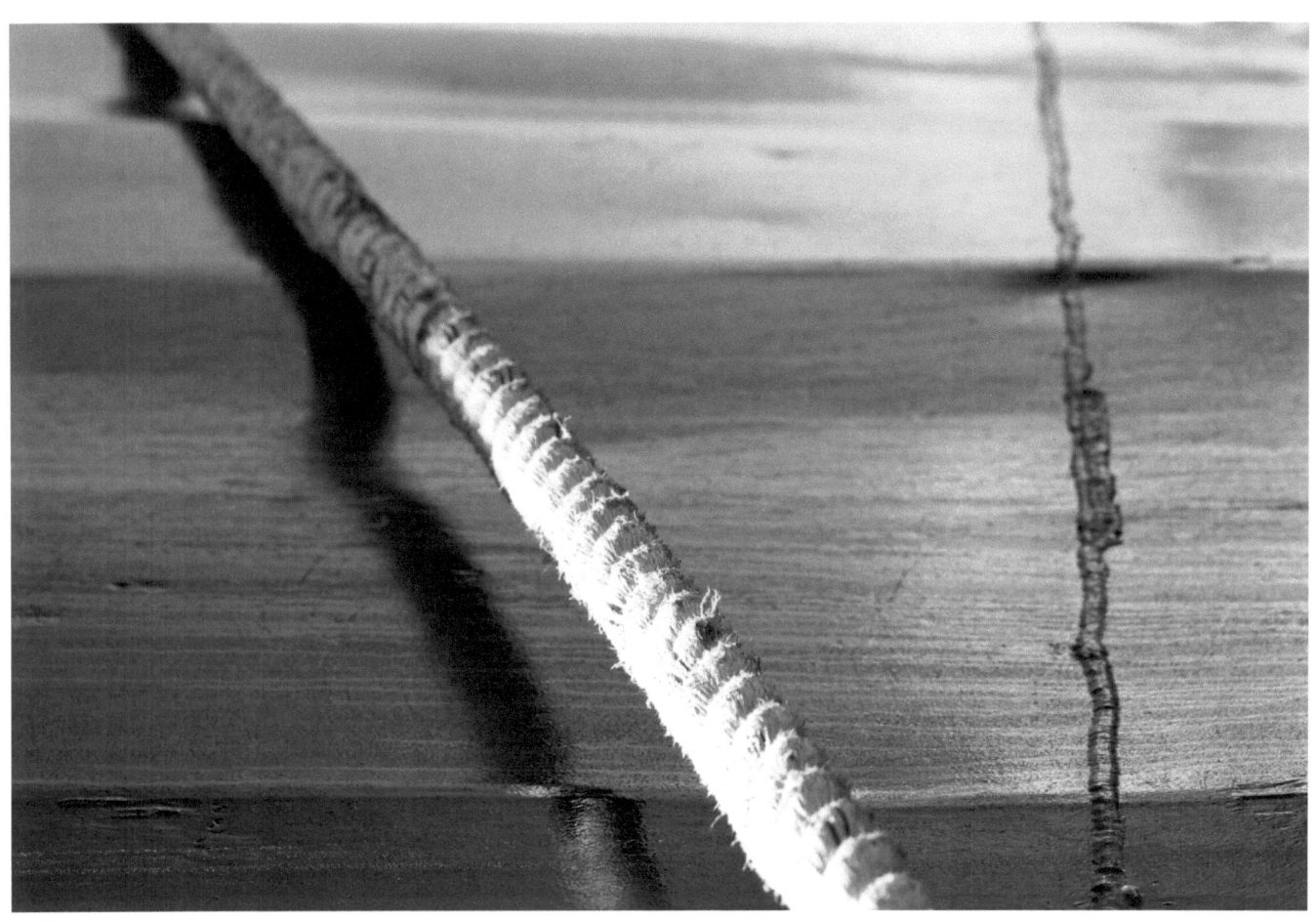

8470

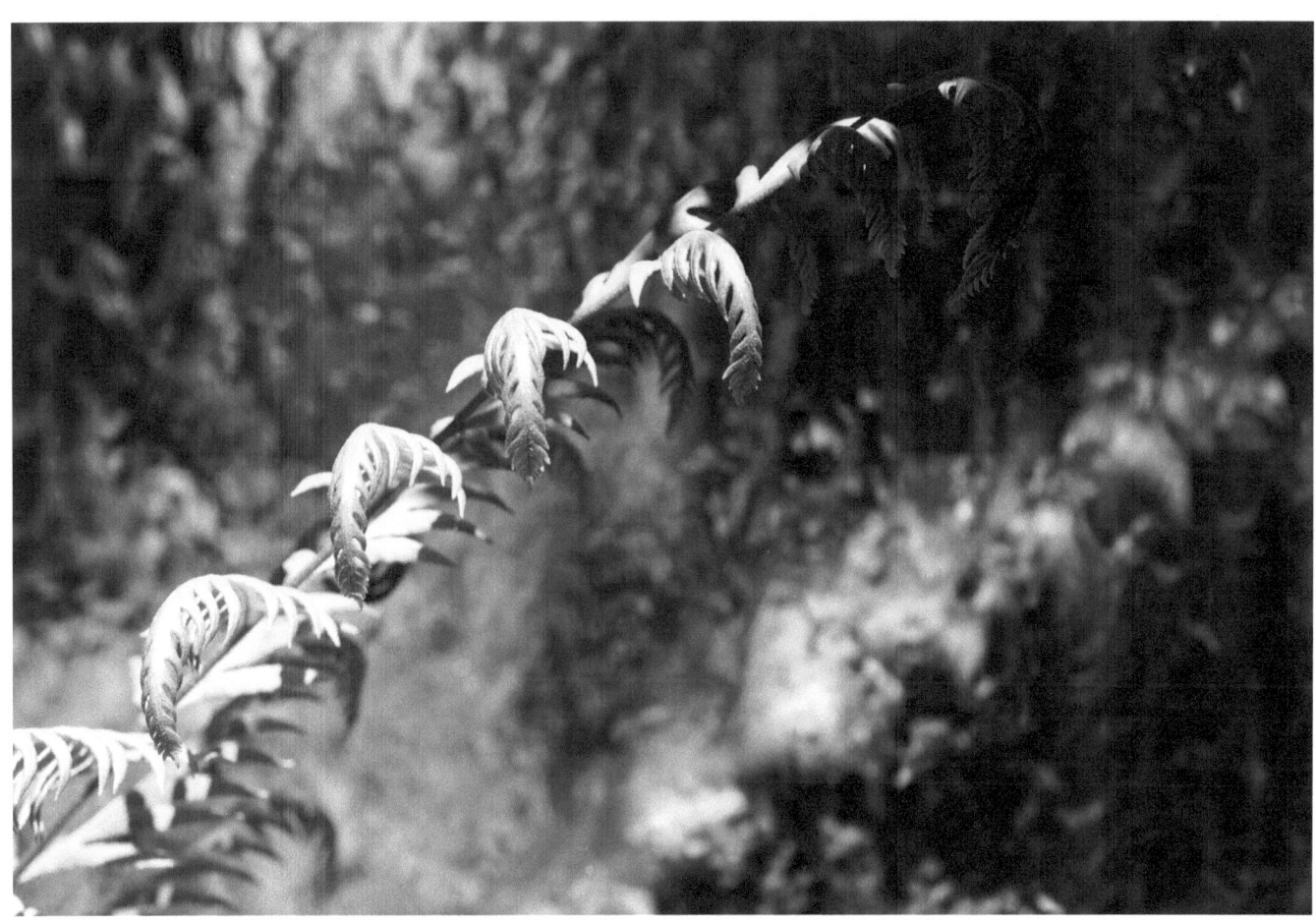

8889

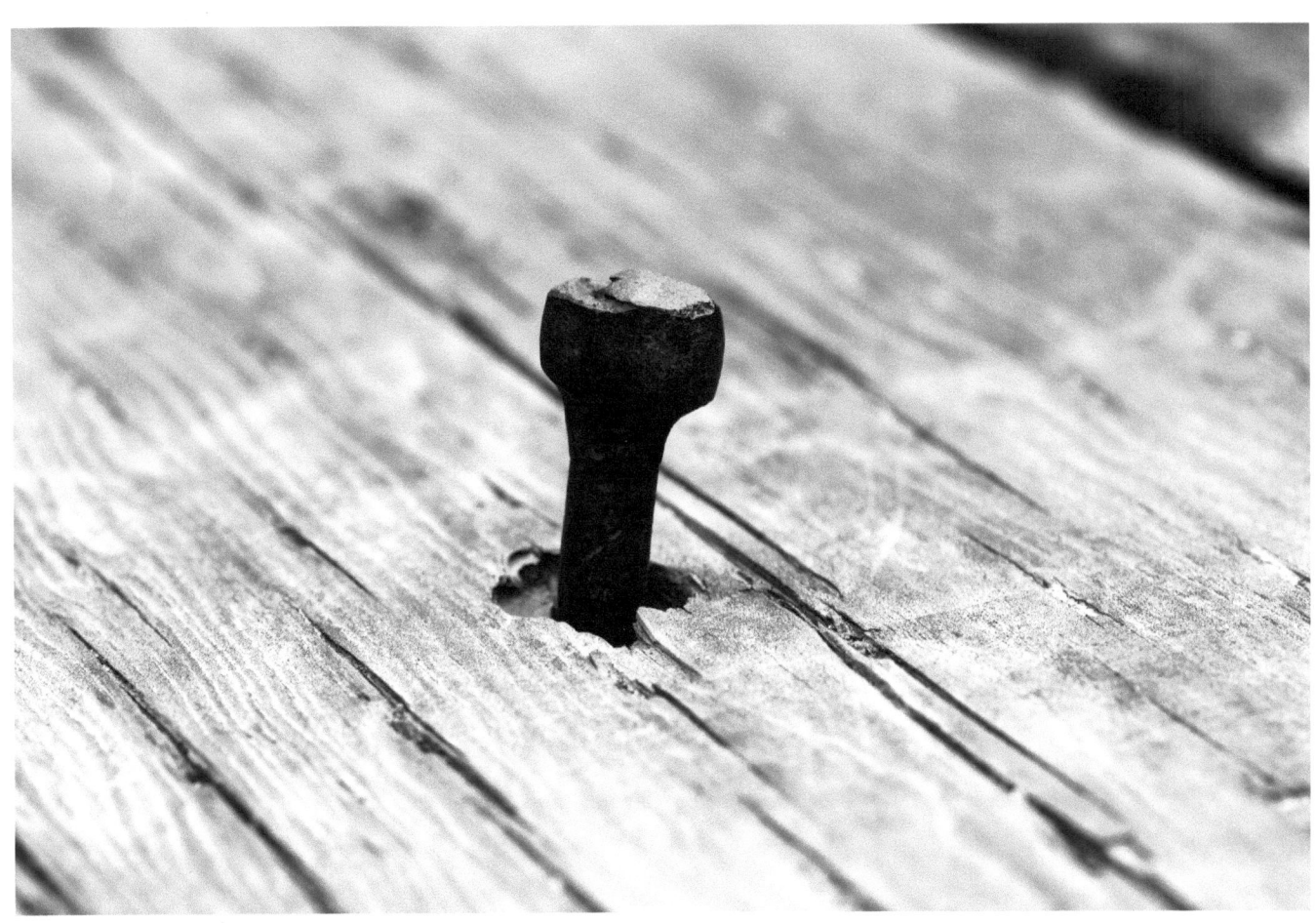

9024

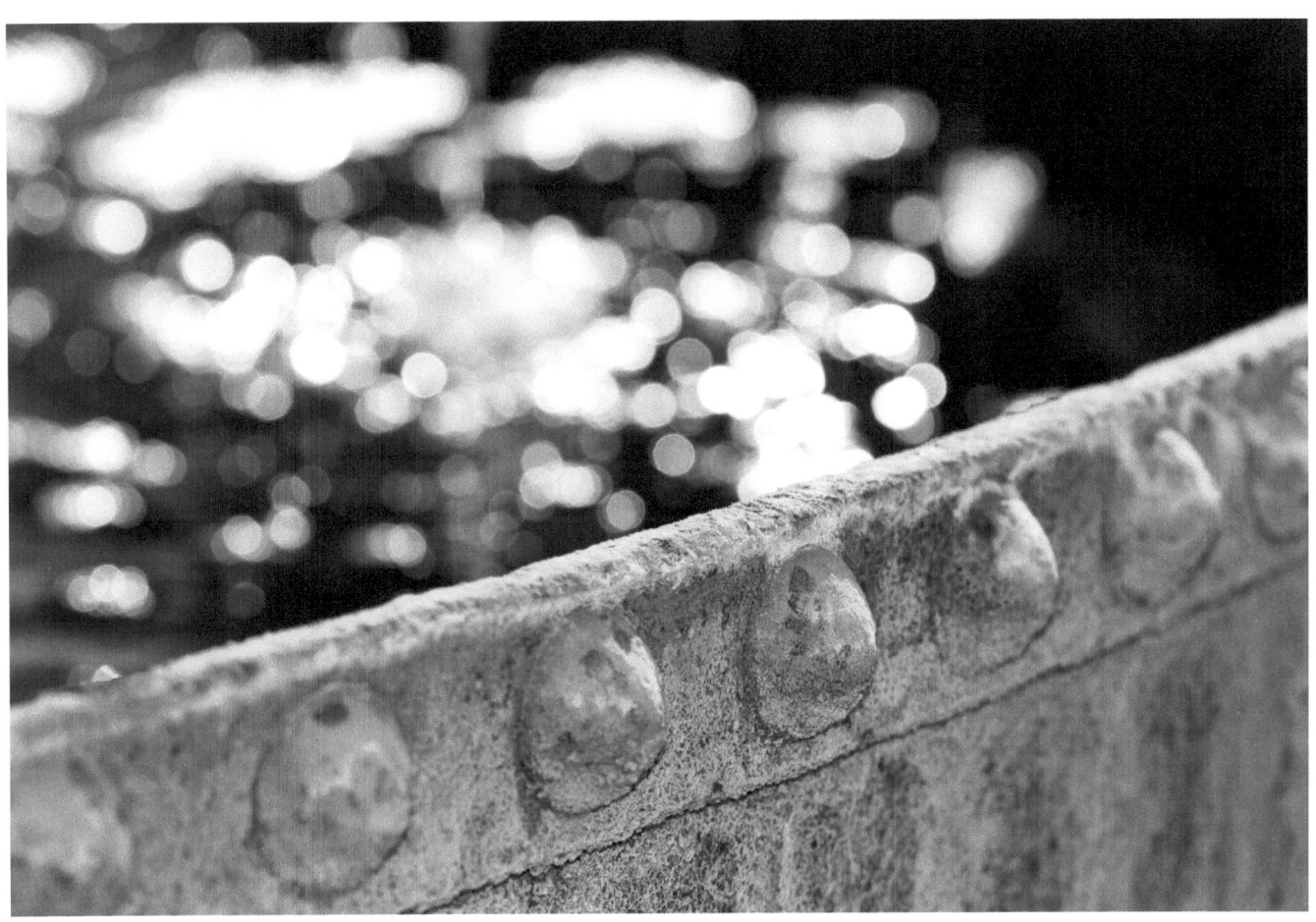

9430

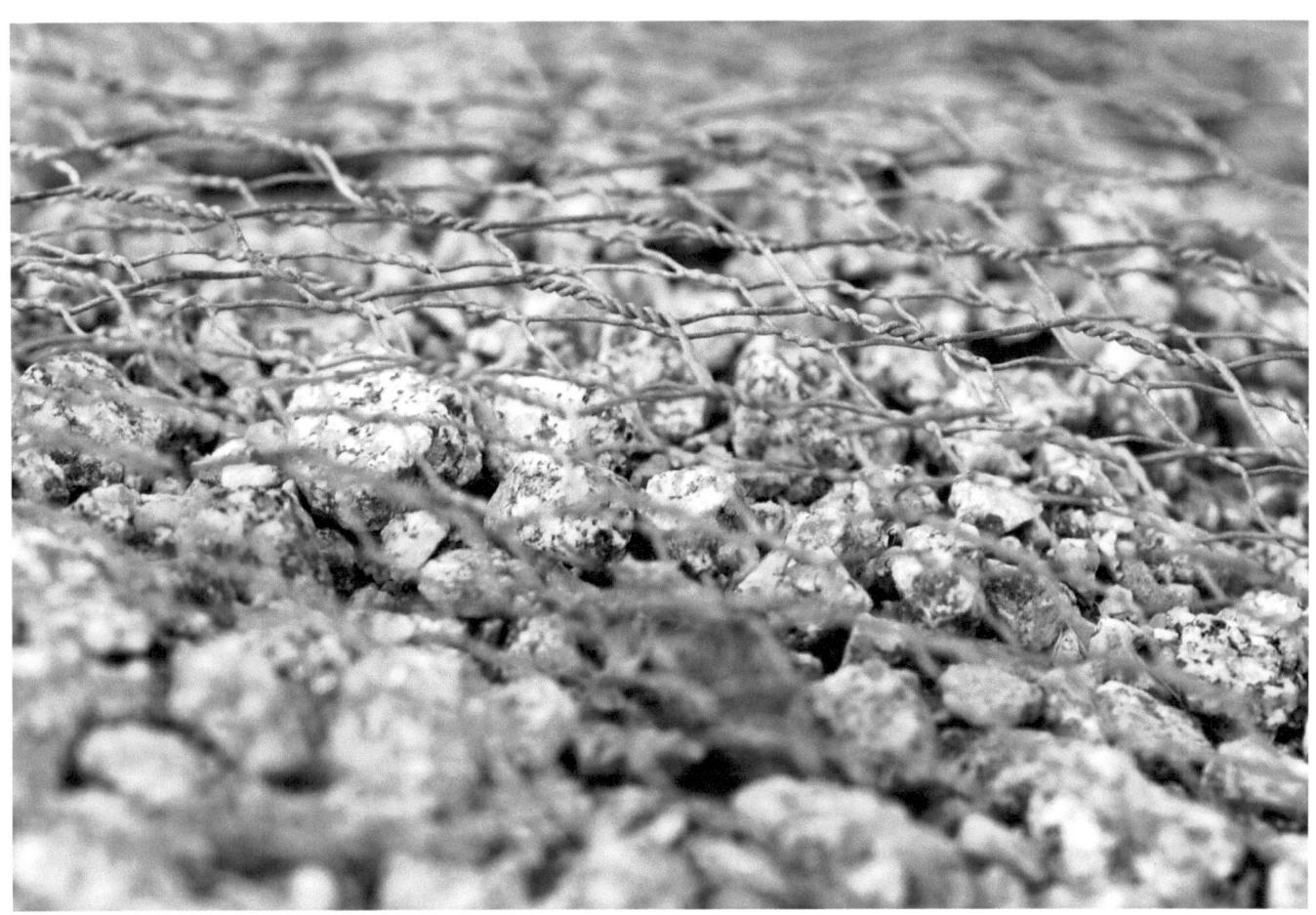

9970

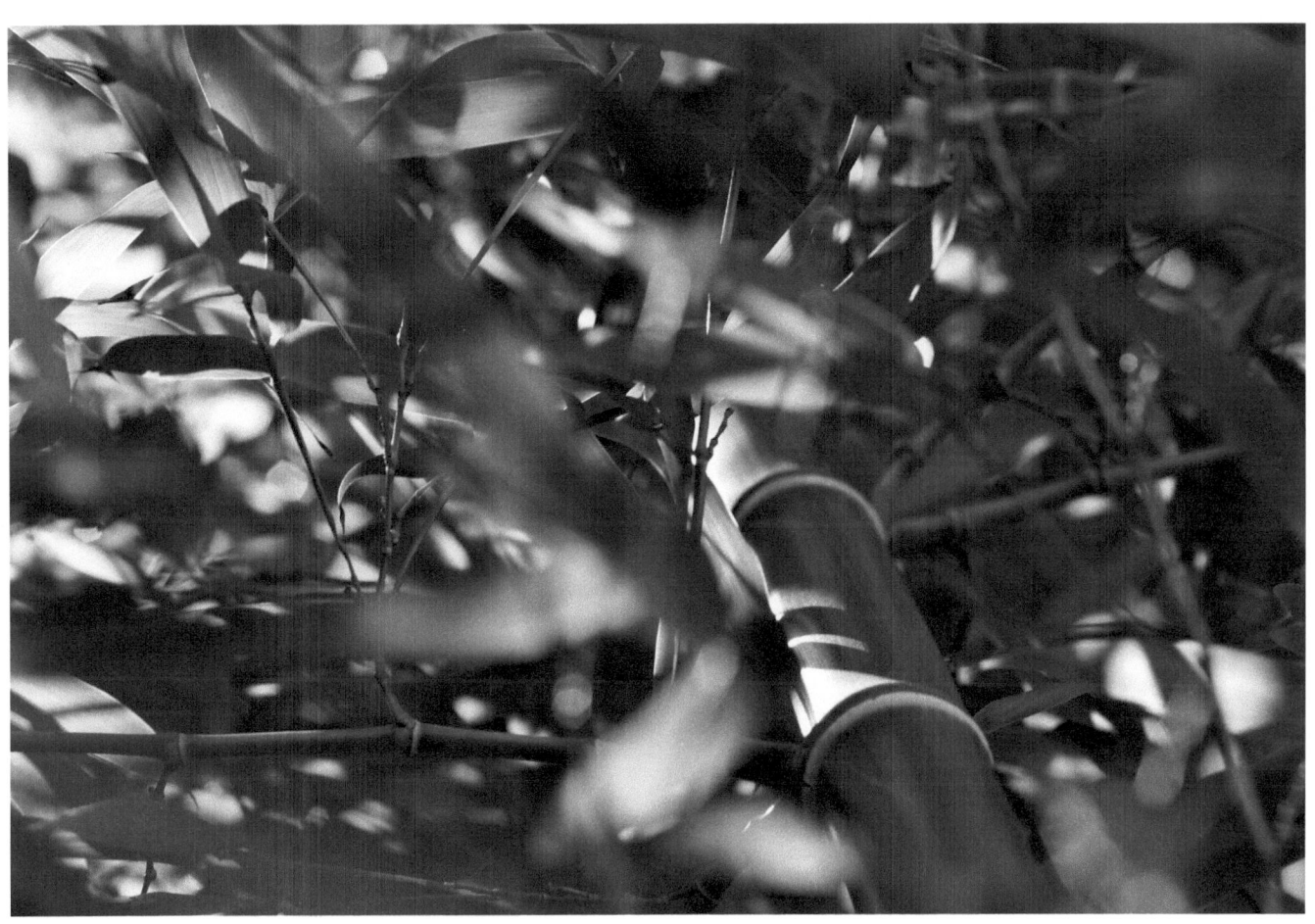

9975

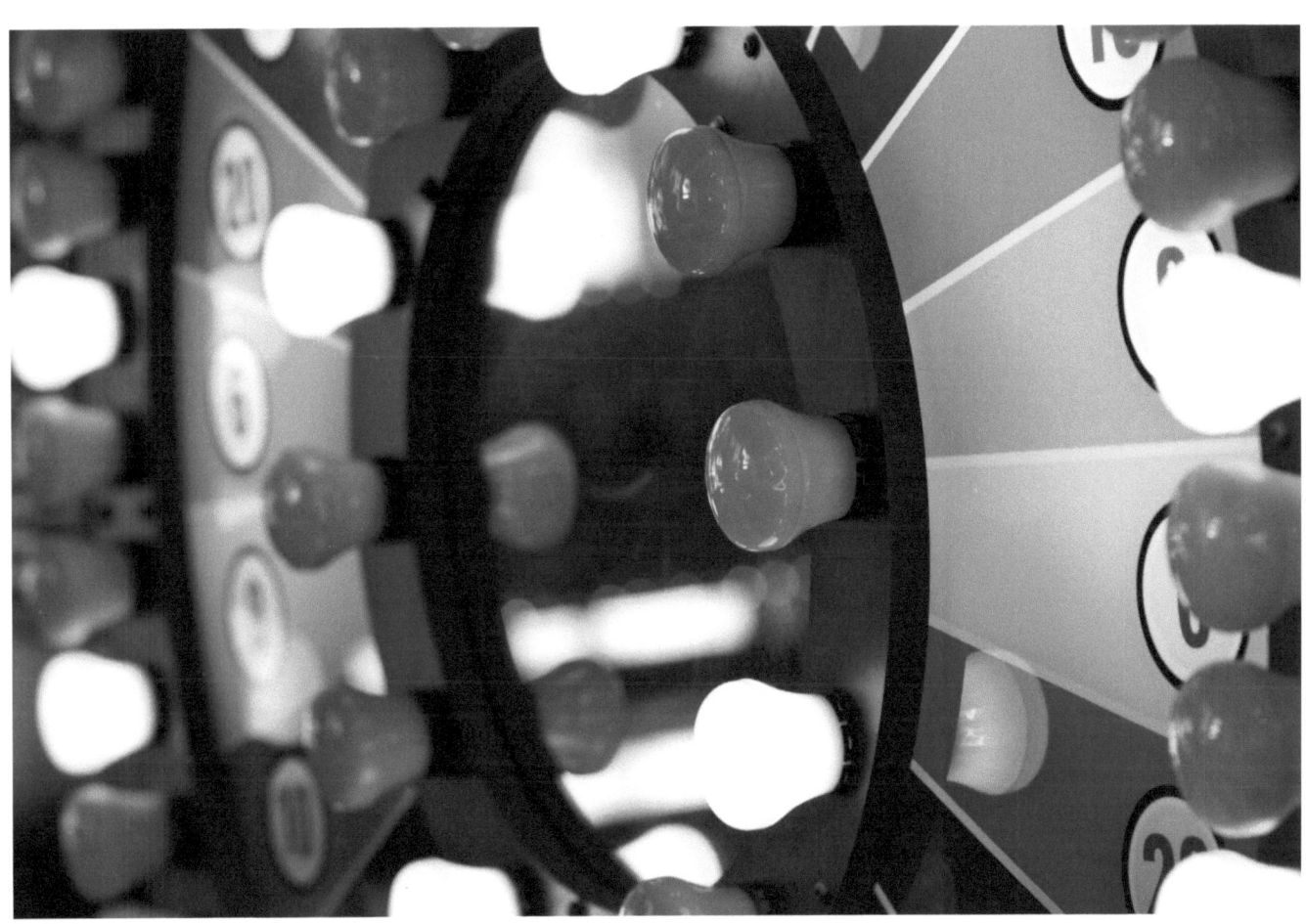

9980

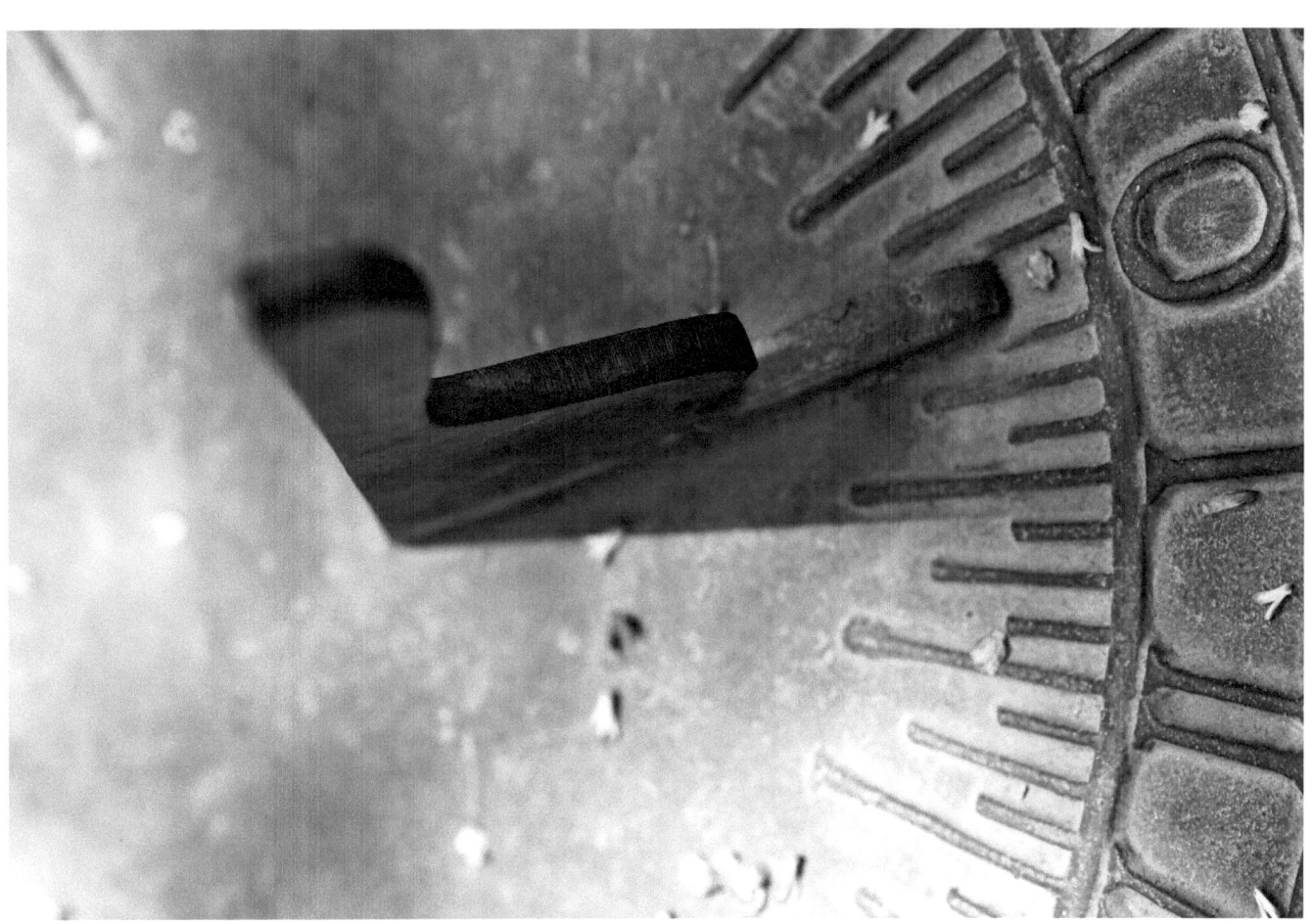

10002